WHAT IS WE?

WHAT IS WE?

Ragini Tharoor Srinivasan

agenda
publishing

First published in 2026 by Agenda Publishing

Agenda Publishing Limited
PO Box 185
Newcastle upon Tyne
NE20 2DH

www.agendapub.com

ISBN 978-1-78821-836-8 (hardcover)
ISBN 978-1-78821-837-5 (paperback)

British Library Cataloguing-in-Publication Data
A catalogue record for this book is
available from the British Library

Typeset by Patty Rennie

Printed and bound in the UK by
CPI Group (UK) Ltd, Croydon, CR0 4YY

EU GPSR authorised representative
Logos Europe, 9 rue Nicolas Poussin
17000 La Rochelle, France
contact@logoseurope.eu

But who is this “we”? / Is it even possible to form a “we”? / Is that even the question?

Claudia Rankine

It is the task of the imagination to place a question mark upon the declarative.

Gayatri Chakravorty Spivak

Contents

Acknowledgments

This book would not have been written without Chi Rainer Bornfree's vital provocation: "What question should we ask when we are questioning power?" Anthony Morgan heard my first attempt at a response and invited me to develop this book, in the spirit of "The New Basics." I'm tremendously grateful to Chi and Anthony, and to Steven Gerrard of Agenda, for giving me the opportunity to ask and reask and keep asking my title question.

This book reflects many conversations and experiences I have had over the years, and many friends and colleagues whose work I have been privileged to read, and many smart folks whose questions and words underpin my own. My special thanks to my students at the University of Nevada, Reno, the University of Arizona, and Rice University; my colleagues at *India Currents*; and Reid Gómez, R. Radhakrishnan, Michael Schwarz, Carly Thomsen, and Rabbit Varela.

I've taken liberties with my family here and elsewhere, especially my parents, my in-laws, and my children. I hope they know why, and how grateful I am. Seamus Murphy shared his illuminating vision – a photo of one of the final frames of Hany Abu-Assad's *Paradise Now*, taken from the audience during the film's world premiere at the Berlinale 2005 – for the cover of this book. Brandon Levin read the manuscript at various stages, and knows by heart all the words that exist between the lines.

For whatever it's worth, B, this little book is for you. No I without we. Or, you know, something like that.

Introduction: "We" is a method

This book offers a simple answer to a simple question.

What is "we"?

"We" – I propose – is a method. Not a *who* to be specified. Not a collective to join or from which to be expelled. "We" is a method: a technique; a procedure; a means to some end (actually, many ends); a craft; a systematic mode of arrangement. "We" is a method through which the world is structured and ordered, from the micro-unit of "we two"[1] to the macro-units of geopolitical or even interspecies alliance. As a method, "we" can be repeated – and is – with varying degrees of intentionality. As a method, "we" conscripts and recruits, sometimes frankly, sometimes slyly. "We" is a method that underpins the ordering structures of our selves, our societies, and our worlds.

Which means, of course, that there is nothing simple about it.

What is "we"? According to the *Oxford English Dictionary*, "we" is "the subjective case of the first-person plural pronoun." It is a pronoun "used indefinitely in general statements in which the speaker or writer includes those addressed, i.e., his or her contemporaries, compatriots, fellow human beings, etc." Dictionary.com defines "we" simply as the "nominative plural of I."

"We" is not just me, not just you, not just I, but rather me-*plus*, you-*plus*, I-*plus*. I-pluralized. More than me. When queried, ChatGPT writes that "we" wouldn't earn a player many Scrabble points, but it is nevertheless a "common and essential word in English for expressing group membership . . . a fundamental part of language used to talk about ourselves in relation to others."

"We." The word is so fundamental, so obvious, that it is, to borrow writer Amit Chaudhuri's description of the obvious, "disorienting... hidden by habits of individual, collective, and institutional thinking." But – and this is the premise of this short book – if we confront it, if we stay with the obvious, if we turn it around and defamiliarize it from all angles, pronounce it ten different ways, until it sounds like a word that's never been said before, it might have "a surreal – even a spiritual – power."[2]

"We."

"We" is something we do even when we don't (say it, that is). I am an English professor. When I type those five words, I am already activating more than one "we": professors; English professors specifically; teachers more generally; the English, whoever they are; and English, whatever that is. This, after all, is what any statement of identity – any "I am" statement – is. It is an evocation of a "we" in whose terms said identity is legible. Even the statement "I am an individual" is, ironically, a "we" statement, since an "individual" is only identifiable as such in relation to a group from which the individual is being distinguished. To write about "we" as method is thus to write about a method of *identification* – even if and when it takes a negative, or dis-identificatory, form, and even if "we" has not technically been specified at all.

"We" is a "performative utterance" in linguist J. L. Austin's terms, in which "to *say* something is to *do* something; or in which *by* saying or *in* saying something we are doing something."[3] Following Austin, to say "we" is to perform, not just describe. By writing "we" and in pronouncing "we" something is done, enacted, and carried out. A context is opened up, a condition is inaugurated, and a collectivity is assumed or sundered. A new rhetorical situation emerges, in which "we" has been uttered, whether explicitly or implicitly. Thus, "we" sets up or even changes the rules of the game.

"We" is something we routinely "get away with." "Getting away with things is essential," Austin writes.[4]

Unless, of course, we don't (get away with it, that is).

Consider an early scene in Zadie Smith's novel *Swing Time*, in which the unnamed narrator, the child of a black Jamaican woman and a white British man, shows her white classmate, Lily, a copy of the 1943 American musical film *Stormy Weather*. Lily is offended by the film's all-black cast: "It was unkind, [Lily] said, to have only black people in a film, it wasn't fair. Maybe in America you could do that, but not here, in England, where everybody was equal . . . We wouldn't like that, would we?"

Walking home, the narrator wonders: "what [could Lily] have meant by the word 'we'?"[5]

Lily didn't get away with it.

"We."

Swing Time is written in the first person about "we's" on multiple scales, from a pair of childhood best friends, to the global African diaspora, to the politics and confounding flexibility of twenty-first-century biracial and transnational identification. In practice, the entire novel unfolds a version of the question that the young narrator asks herself in that early scene. What was Lily attempting to do in that moment with "we"? How was she, the narrator, supposed to respond? What does anyone ever mean by "we" – this term that is "too loaded to use un-self-consciously," in feminist scholar Robyn Maynard's words?[6]

By placing the two letters in quotation marks, Smith performs the operation with which I have also now begun this book: the act of distinguishing the word – we – from the idea of the word: "we." This initial act of demarcation by inverted commas transforms we into an object of inquiry: "we." In what follows, I further specify "we" as method, by demonstrating that "we" is not just an object of potential knowledge but also a means of transforming knowledge production itself.

The gap between specifying "we" as object and "we" as method – between "we" as a quantity to be known and "we" as a mode of meaning making – is central to this book's structure and arguments. Before "we" can serve as a method, it must be recognized conceptually, in a broad range of guises, and in distinct scenes of operation. To adapt the words of Kuan-Hsing Chen, a leading scholar of Inter-Asian cultural studies, I propose that "[we] as *method* recognizes the need to keep a critical distance from uninterrogated *notions* of [we]."[7] Each of the following chapters therefore interrogates a notion of "we" that is operative in a particular context. At the same time, each explores how enlisting "we" as method might then illuminate our understandings of that context.

In his seminal *Asia as Method*, Chen offers "method" as "a critical proposition to transform the existing knowledge structure and at the same time to transform ourselves."[8] Building on the work of cultural theorists Takeuchi Yoshimi and Mizoguchi Yuzo, Chen theorizes "Asia as method" as a practice of Asian societies "meeting" elsewhere than they have met before. The goal is that they then develop newly self-reflexive conceptions of history, the world, the West, each other, and themselves. The operative word here is "self-reflexive." The signal purpose of using Asia as method is "so that the understanding of the self may be transformed, and subjectivity rebuilt."[9]

And so it is with "we": It, too, is a self-reflexive method through which our understandings of self and subjectivity may be rebuilt.

I noted already that I am an English professor. More specifically, I teach Asian American, South Asian Anglophone, and world literatures – primarily of the twentieth and twenty-first centuries – as well as critical ethnic, feminist, and postcolonial theory and cultural studies, to undergraduate and graduate students in US academe. I'm also a former editor of an Indian American magazine and a freelance essayist, and I work on public discourses and institutional configurations of knowledge, broadly defined. I teach and write about textual and nontextual objects that call into question the distinctions between the particular and the universal, between identity and difference, between the part and the whole, between us scholars and the disciplines in which we work, and between literary texts and the communities they purport to represent.

In simplest terms, I work on the relationship between "I" and "we."

To return to Chen, one of my chief aims in elaborating "we" as method is to investigate "we's" imbrication with "I" and, equally, "I's" overdetermination by "we." In Judith Butler's words, "The 'I' who I am is also to some extent a 'we' even as tensions tend to mark the relation of these two senses of one's life... Others precede me, anticipate me to some degree, and their provisioning and early effects – loving impingements, as it were – start to form this person who eventually comes to refer to itself as 'I.'"[10] Interdependency, dialogue, collectivity, and relationality are thus key, sustained topics of interest throughout this book. So, too, is intertextuality, as I strive for a citational practice that deemphasizes my own authorial mastery and instead foregrounds my efforts at playful, critical, creative engagement with other writers, thinkers, and scholars.

With respect to the intertextual, I should note that in the months that I was writing the first draft of this book, I was finalizing edits on two others, each of which has left a mark on the following pages. The first, *The End Doesn't Happen All at Once*, is an epistolary memoir about friendship, change, and the loss of collective possibility that I co-wrote with Chi Rainer Bornfree during the first four years of the Covid pandemic.[11] That book primarily unfolds in the first and second person, but it begins with a short prologue written from the vantage of "we." Writing the dozens of pages that were ultimately condensed into the prologue, along with co-writing the book proposals that had to represent both of our perspectives, were for me the most challenging parts of our collaboration. Chi and my battle to arrive at a narrative "we" mirrored the collective struggle to consolidate a sociological "we" that could truly band together in the global fight against Covid, as I discuss in Chapter 5. Moreover, the epistolary form of the text meant that each of our "I's" only ever emerged in address and relation to the other's, complicating conventional ideas of singular perspective and individual voice, as discussed in Chapter 3.

The second book is a scholarly monograph, *Overdetermined*, in which I examine how Indian English literatures and authors are enlisted in US university classrooms in particular debates on ethnic identity, postcolonial histories, and the global system of the Anglophone.[12] That book is interested in what teachers and writers, students and readers, *do* with literature, and what we individually and collectively want from literature, over and above what any literary text can say in and of itself.

For starters, one of the things many readers want from literature is that it represents us; we want to see ourselves in certain texts. Or, to put that differently, we want to be hailed into the collectivity that "comes into existence" through "the textual encounter."[13] For example, we hope that an Indian poem might have some fidelity to what we take to be Indian experience, or that an African American novel gives voice to what we recognize as an African American community.[14] By that same token, one of the things that writers of literature chafe against the most is the burden of representing their so-called communities.

This is a deeply familiar circuit – from the reader's desire for representation, to the writer's resistance to the burden of that demand – and it overdetermines the representational work that any literary text itself can or cannot do. As scholar Mark Chiang provocatively puts it in the Asian American context, Asian American literature will always "'[fail] to stand for' Asian Americans," because it is always being judged in terms of its referential relation to a collectivity it can never totally represent.[15]

In spring 2019, inspired by Chiang, I asked my undergraduate literature students to write a "nonrepresentative representation" of a community to which they belonged. It could be anything: the community of students, Asians, Americans, twins, ice-skaters, video-gamers, you name it. The students were perplexed, so I doubled down. Write a text, I said, that does or says that which it cannot do or say. Find a way to mark the limits of an attempt to "speak for" both yourself and others. Write some "we" through your "I," I urged them. Every representation, every locution, every word comes up against the limits of referentiality, so just write! But they were still anxious. After all, in asking them to produce a "nonrepresentative representation," I had essentially asked them to fail. *Overdetermined* explores this manner of failure and the fiction and scholarship produced in its wake. Chapters 1 and 7 of this book pursue similar issues, by discussing the "we's" of ethnicity and race.

What is "we"? I am deliberately posing the question like that, as opposed to more familiar versions of it, such as "who is 'we'?" as political philosopher Hans Bernhard Schmid asks.[16] Or, "who are we?" to quote literary theorist Gayatri Chakravorty Spivak.[17] Such questions assume that "we" already *are*; we just need to be specified, qualified, and described.[18] I am not convinced. The question, I argue, is not how to develop a vocabulary that is adequate to representing some collectivity but rather how to apprehend the simultaneous violence and vitality of aspirations to collectivity in the first place. The Asian American text always fails to represent Asian Americans; still, it continues to appear in the Asian American literature classroom. "I" cannot speak "we" and yet inevitably I do, with equal parts audacity and hope.

What is "we"? "We" is the desired goal of all political action and organization. It is the ground on and through which subjects come together in knowledge of our shared humanity. At the same time, "we" is a perpetual obstacle to organizing on both small and large scales, because invocations of "we" are always both "parochial and imperialistic," as Schmid writes. "They are parochial in that they fail to recognize some of us as who they are by excluding them from the circle of 'we.' And they are imperialistic in that they conceive of 'everybody' on the model of just some of us, thus marginalizing 'the rest' of us."[19]

"We" is an epistemology. "We" is an assumption of shared subjectivity, perspective, or experience. "We" is a call to affiliate. "We" is an event. "We" is a promise and a threat. "We" is a term that posits and relies upon that which lies outside of its ambit; "we" always refers to "not-we." It is therefore determined by its constitutive exterior: all those elements that by definition cannot be "we," specifically so that "we" are. Mobilizations of "we" are central to operations of power and the possibility of critically interrogating its operations. As feminist theorist Robyn Wiegman writes, "we" is a "towering inferno of universalism" and "monstrous display of self-infatuation" – an error, an excess – that we can nevertheless not not want, a "tantalizing hallucination" we cannot help but desire.[20]

That said, "we" is not merely a concept-metaphor for an object of desire whose boundaries give way as soon as it comes into view. Rather, "we" is a method through which the slippage of boundaries is enacted, apprehended, and instrumentalized. "We" can be royal or editorial, and to that end formal and distancing. "We" can also be familial and familiar, and to that end intimate and inviting. "We" is totalizing ambition and intellectual humility and a feminist method of situating knowledge.[21]

"We" is central to our shared vocabulary as humanists, and it underlies the very premise of our having a shared vocabulary in the first place. But, again, "we" has been so overdetermined by the question of "who" and the problem of adjudicating responses to that question that its basic operations remain undertheorized.

I began this Introduction by noting that this book offers a simple answer to a simple question – and then I recanted that description. Already it should be clear that there is nothing "simple" about "we," nothing simple about a concept so "fundamental" – beyond the fact that it merits deep scrutiny, now more than ever.

Writing about the legacy of the Covid pandemic, novelist Elif Shafak observes that we in the 2020s are living through a "crisis of meanings." We had been collectively consulting "the same old leather-bound dictionary that was for the most part compiled in the aftermath of the Cold War," she writes, but the pandemic set our metaphorical dictionary aflame.[22]

> We assumed we had the proper definitions of all these core concepts, mostly thanks to the generations that preceded us, who had done the hard work. We surmised that we would never have to deal with 'the basics' as we were far beyond that historical stage. But now, with a half-destroyed dictionary in our hands, we need to sit down and rethink the entries.[23]

According to Shafak, the "simplest" terms will be "hardest" to redefine: terms such as democracy, happiness, normal.[24] And, I submit: *we*.

That said, these pages aim not at resolution or, pace Shafak, definition, but rather at the perpetual renewal of critical inquiry. In the chapters to come, I offer many provisional answers to my suggestive, titular question; equally, the question will change form, sometimes right when an answer appears to be within grasp. To some readers, it might feel that I am offering no answers at all. Bear with me, please. I offer "What is we?" as what scholar-novelist Saikat Majumdar calls a "teaching question": a question that is "big and sweeping" and that "drive[s] a passion for learning and provide[s] an understanding of the discipline in a historical capacity."[25] I propose that it is a worthy task to hear, read, and think the question of "we" – never mind settle it! In the process, we will grasp its myriad reverberations and implications. "What is we?" thus drives this book's inquiry forward, while each chapter's distinct point of entry opens the question up further, transforming "we" while exploring its many contours and attendant discourses.

Each of my ten chapters elaborates "we" as a particular form of method. Some accounts are retrospective: how "we" has been used to do *x*. Some are prospective: how "we" might otherwise be used. None are normative. Even those chapters that trace "we" as a method of communion, liberation, and remembering are exploratory, speculative – again, not arguments for how "we" must serve as method, but rather accounts of how it might. Each chapter explores the tension between intentional uses of "we," on the one hand, and those that reveal a subject's ideological conscription into some "we," on the other. The chapters are paired and unfold through antonymic relations. My aim in organizing the book this way is to amplify the nuance, complexity, and range of operations of "we" as a concept that can always be used to do, or made to mean, the opposite of what it says on the tin.

Chapters 1 and 2 elaborate "we" as a method of *inclusion* and *exclusion*, a method through which boundaries are both erased and established. "We" can be a way to assert the bonds of ethnic community: for instance, through recognition of a shared palate or soundscape, or via the familiarizing force of accent.[26] "We" is also an anti-communal mode of privatizing care and apportioning labor through the construct of the nuclear family.[27]

Chapters 3 and 4 investigate *communion* and *isolation*. "We," I demonstrate with respect to the example of epistolary poetry, is a method of writerly collaboration that provincializes, transcends, and yet also deepens the first-person narrative voice. At the same time, "we" is an antisocial method of distancing, exemplified by the ironically alienating effects of contemporary information technologies, digital communication, and social media.

"We," I show in Chapter 5, can be a method of *coercion* and gaslighting, as in the pernicious pandemic-era refrain "we have the tools" – which flies in the face of the reality of global vaccine apartheid and the privatization of Covid therapeutics. By that same token, Chapter 6 offers, "we" might become a method of *liberation* in the quest for reproductive freedom, if abortion narratives can be deindividualized and reframed as a matter of shared responsibility and destiny.

In Chapters 7 and 8, "we" emerges as a method of *division* in which histories of difference structure the racial imaginary of the present, erecting insuperable boundaries between self and other. At the same time, it is a method of *incorporation* in which the other is cannibalized, whether selfishly or altruistically.

Finally, Chapters 9 and 10 offer "we" as a method of *forgetting* and *remembering*. "We" is a method of forgetting that underpins national imagining, since, in order to come together as "we the people" with a shared present and future, we have to forget the many pasts that we do not share.[28] Equally, "we" is a method of remembering history, ancestors, gods, land, and earth – nothing less, in other words, than who "we" are or might yet be.

Beyond offering "we" as a method, I seek with these ten chapters to demonstrate how traditional forms of disciplinary knowledge both enable and constrain the audiences we do and do not address. As method, "we" is an invitation to elaborate all knowledge in terms of its largest possible sphere of address. At the same time, "we" is an acknowledgment of all knowledge's historical contingency, partiality, and limits. To this end, I argue that "we" is a species of praxis: a simultaneous mode of meaning making and doing, which stands to elucidate forms of social relations while, at the same time, transforming them.[29]

I also seek to think with and between social, historical, political, grammatical, linguistic, and personal methods of analysis, frames of reference, and rubrics. This book is therefore willfully trans- and cross-disciplinary. My chapters are rooted in and routed through readings of literary, theoretical, and philosophical texts, contemporary events and politics, journalistic and public discourse, and research in Asian American, South Asian Anglophone, ethnic, and postcolonial literary and cultural studies. Throughout, the American context and US example are emphasized, not because they are exemplary, but because that is the critical location and institutional ground of this writing and my own training.

More than one chapter makes reference to – and in some cases offers sustained discussion of – a text I previously wrote or argument I previously made and now have occasion to revisit. I take this approach because every argument carries within it a biography of thought, and the feminist tradition of situating knowledges requires surfacing this biography. I aim to channel the spirit of what my colleague Kiese Laymon calls "the rugged majesty of revision."[30] After all, as a college professor of mine used to say, there is no thinking without writing, and no writing without rewriting.

Some readers may class this book as a para-academic or semi-public work. Others might be satisfied that it is simply an extended essay on "we," no qualification necessary. You may have found this work because it's part of a series in public philosophy. For my part, I will say that it is an attempt to think critically and carefully about a subject I have come to believe subtends almost all others: our ability to be, address, and relate beyond the self.

In elaborating "we" as a method along these lines, my hope is to reissue the challenge of failure that I set my students and address it to a wider audience. I seek to encourage readers to rise to the possibility of impossibility, and to concede at the outset the hallucinatory quality of the aspiration of the universal. "We" is immeasurably larger than we think it is. It is also much smaller than we hope.

Evie Shockley's 2023 poetry collection *Suddenly We* begins with a picture of a "we" composed of 43 "you's" and one "me," which visualizes "we" as a purposeful mode of construction. For Shockley, the image represents an unrealized dream of "greater collectivity."[31] I read it as a warning that "we" might always and at any time be deconstructed. "We" is a tower from which "me" might easily be ejected and every "you" replaced or supplanted by another, by "they" or "I." It is a reminder that every mode of making "we" is subject to unmaking, and remaking, and making and unmaking anew.

"We" is what we write toward. Equally, "we" is what we may never reach.

And so: we keep writing.

1

Of inclusion

> The real question is not how to get beyond identity, but rather how to get to it in the first place . . .
>
> David Palumbo-Liu[1]

Before I knew what community was – what it can, might, and should be – I thought it was my job to resist it.

I was 22 years old and about to assume the editorship of an Indian American monthly magazine called *India Currents*. It was July 2007, and the magazine, founded in San Jose, California, was two decades old.[2] When I got to my desk on my first day, I learned that I had inherited all the feature stories and op-eds that my predecessor, Ashok Jethanandani, had lined up for the August issue. Ashok had planned a cover story on the India Community Center in Milpitas, California, which was then (and remains) the largest Indian community center in North America.[3]

I didn't want to run a story about a community center. I had just written an undergraduate honors thesis on the trap of ethnic identification, and assuming the mantle of ethnic magazine editor had already sent me into a state of cognitive dissonance. But I didn't have a choice. Editor of a community magazine apparently meant editor of a cover story on a community center.

In the editorial column I wrote for that issue, I tried to articulate the ambivalence I felt about both the institutional formation of the "community center" and the premise of "community" itself. I titled my editorial "Call it Community."[4] It began like this:

> As a student of literary and cultural theory, I have been trained to be suspicious of the word "community." Sure, the term is acceptably used in conversation, but when held up to critical scrutiny, it has little resonance.
>
> Imagine the following scene. A guest lecturer stands at the front of a classroom, delivering a talk on South Asian writers in the post-colonial context. All is well – we students are taking notes, listening attentively – until the lecturer says something like this: "Arundhati Roy's Booker Prize brought pride to her own community." Or, "female characters in Indian diasporic fiction are subject to their community's patriarchal values."
>
> All heads lift from notebooks; our pens drop in dismay. We have found the speaker's Achilles Heel, the lynchpin that will unravel this painstakingly constructed theoretical elaboration. The lecturer has used one of the most contentious terms of all – "community" – as shorthand for far more complex populations and ideas. After all, who comprises Roy's "community"? How can anyone attempt to speak for diverse populations, distinct individuals, and multiple forms of alliance with that watered-down, over-used term?

"Suspicious." "Critical." "Dismay." "Contentious." Nearly two decades after I wrote those words, I'm struck by just how embattled I was about the concept of community. The operative word here is *concept* – in contradistinction to the *experience* of community with which I should have been intimately familiar. My immigrant mother and father had moved to the United States from India as an undergraduate and graduate student, respectively, and they settled in northern California in the early 1980s. There, they were part of – equally, they were part of building – a community of other Indian American immigrants and their children, among whom my brother and I grew up.

To be sure, our Indian American community was not homogenous. It included Hindus, Muslims, and Christians. It included speakers of languages including Bengali, Gujarati, Hindi, Malayalam, Marathi, Punjabi, Swahili, Tamil, and Urdu. It included diasporic subjects whose migratory itineraries had taken them through East Africa, England, and multiple regions of the United States. It included all different levels of education and a variety of professions.

Equally, the Indian American milieu was not our only experience of community. We belonged to a multiracial, multiethnic, secular school community, as well as a neighborhood community, and various other micro-communities organized around extracurricular activities and arts.

All that aside, we had one primary community, and it was legibly "Indian."

In practice, community meant that there were always adults other than my parents who fed and watered us and drove us around. Community meant Friday evening after-school teas that extended into dinners and dance parties in homes that were as familiar as our own. Community meant singing along to Bollywood songs despite not knowing the words and arguing over which aunty made the best pooris. Community meant coming of age among others; it meant having one's growth seen, supported, and celebrated. Equally, it meant having witnesses to one's transgressions and failures, missteps and errant phases. From your first birthday, to your fortieth. From your wedding, to your funeral. Community meant that there were those with whom you shared a past and those with whom you might expect to experience the future.

* * *

Community: "a body of people viewed collectively"; "the people as a group"; "the body of people having common or equal rights or rank."

Community is a structure of belonging and recognition, and it can refer to collective identification in essentially any terms: the coincidence of ethnic or racial identity; shared interests or hobbies; overlapping territory; joint practices or rituals. To be in community is to be with and among others. To be not-alone, not-one, not-I. To adapt Rabindranath Tagore's words, community is connection: "to know another as our very own, and to know ourselves as if we were another's."[5] To be in community is to be "we."

So why was it that I, writing that editorial in 2007, didn't recognize "community" as the enabling substrate it is? Why was I not sufficiently aware of what I myself had lived and experienced? To put a finer point on it, what did I find so alarming about the concept of community? Why was I menaced by the threat of being "we"?

In retrospect, community posed two distinct problems for me: first, an ontological problem of identity; second, an epistemological problem of knowledge. To assume "community," I feared, was to participate in a politically suspect "identity politics"; thus, my editorial column's elaboration of a hypothetical pedagogical misfire in which a professor's assumptions about an author's readership ("Roy's own community") or a character's social milieu ("their community's values") undermined their explanatory credibility – as if "community" were an error in thinking.

"I have been trained to be suspicious of the word 'community,'" I wrote. Historicizing the emergence of that suspicion, I would now put it this way: I had been asked to unlearn what I already knew. I wasn't alone. Writing in 2000, David Palumbo-Liu observed that the theory wars and canon wars of the 1980s and 1990s had seeded a discernible aversion to the concept of identity, leading to calls, from both right and left, that we get "beyond" identity, over identity politics, and into the realm of the "post-ethnic."[6] Some humanists, such as Walter Benn-Michaels, decried identity's antagonistic relationship to class-based mobilization.[7] Asian American studies scholars working "post-identity" sought to correct for the discursive and political homogenization of a community that had crucially never been *one*.[8] More recently, scholar-activist Keeanga-Yamahtta Taylor has argued that identity politics fails because identity too easily comes to stand in for politics.[9] For Olúfémi Táíwò, the problem is that identity politics too often becomes "deference politics": the practice of passing the mic instead of redistributing resources; of assuming that a brown or black body in the room can sufficiently represent all those brown and black bodies barred entry into it.[10]

Plainly, identity cannot and should not substitute for politics. Representation is no panacea for structural inequity. Identitarian thinking that seeds ethnonationalism, xenophobia, white supremacy, and fascism must be resisted at all costs. But the problem with identity is not identity; the problem with identity is what is done in its name.

Similarly, the problem with community is not community. The problem with community is allowing assumptions about communal being and belonging to substitute for critical thought. "The real question," in Palumbo-Liu's words, cited in the epigraph, "is not how to get beyond identity, but rather how to *get to it* in the first place – how to make the transition from typecasting to a recognizing of, precisely, individual identity?"[11]

As an undergraduate student of critical theory and cultural studies, I had become hyper-attuned to the traps of identitarian and communalist thinking. But, as I sat in the editor's chair at *India Currents*, the arrow of my critical suspicion kept hitting the wrong target. A few days before we went to press with the August 2007 issue, I called my college roommate, Rabbit, and expressed dismay over having to publish the cover story about the community center. Rabbit – a public interest lawyer, housing activist, massage worker, herbalist, and healer – listened to me for a beat before responding in simple, unforgettable words.

"Community," they said, "is what we are working toward."

And "we" is one of the methods we use to get there.

* * *

I want to return now to the project of *India Currents*, which was founded in 1987 by Jethanandani and Arvind Kumar as a resource for "the community." The magazine was envisioned as a repository of information that could be shared and circulated among Indian Americans, and as an outlet through which event organizers, spiritual groups, and arts institutions could connect with potential audiences and constituents. The magazine began as a leaflet-like calendar and expanded over the years into a features and opinions magazine published in two (and for a time, three) monthly editions. For going-on four decades, it has maintained low advertising rates (so as not to deter the mom-and-pop Indian grocer, or the student organizer of a local performance), a free distribution model, and a reliance on freelance contributions to generate editorial content.

As a new editor, I was both discomfited and fascinated by the challenge posed by *India Currents*.[12] In many of my college classes, we had learned to specify the violence of "we": from the violence of Orientalist thinking that shores up the identity of the European *us* against an exotic Eastern *them* over there (discussed in Chapter 8), to the violence of a liberal feminism unable to think critically about ethnic, racial, and religious difference. Now, I was supposed to inhabit a "we," to speak as "we," to create a "we." Were these "we's" all part of one project? Was the ethnic magazine addressing an existing community, or was it trying to create a community through shared narrative and address? What was "we"?

In the United States, ethnic publications such as *India Currents* have historically operated on the logic that the content they produce is that which is being ignored by mainstream media outlets.[13] Their motivation is twofold: to profile individuals, highlight achievements, and circulate ideas which would otherwise never be published, and to inculcate in their readers the belonging, pride, and recognition that supposedly cannot be achieved through the consumption of mainstream media. Ethnic publications thus demarcate territory according to the perceived need for coverage of their minority communities. This need is given many alibis: our young people need "role models"; we must be able to "see ourselves" in the faces on television and in newspapers; the dominant culture does not value our achievements, dances, movies, books, religions, and successes. We must "tell the stories" that wouldn't otherwise be told. *Our* stories.[14]

By that same token, and as I learned on the job, ethnic publications such as *India Currents* are never simply engaged in community boosterism. Yes, they do some amount of cheerleading for community members who have achieved public recognition: from spelling bee winners to newly anointed Silicon Valley CEOs.

But their overarching goals are more complex and distinct. I would delineate them thus:

- *to serve the community* that is simultaneously addressed and called into being;
- *to build solidarity* among readers, who are hailed into recognition of themselves, as well as into practices and activities that lead to identification with fellow community members;
- *to instill self-respect* in the community by fostering pride and investment in the achievements of fellow community members;
- *to teach* both community and non-community members about the community's history, concerns, ambitions, and collective goals;
- *to correct* the record by countering misrepresentations and misperceptions of the community, especially those circulated by dominant media outlets.

During my editorship, I was tasked with pursuing these five goals, although it took me some time to consciously articulate them. Every time I accepted or assigned a story, I had to be prepared to answer my publisher Vandana Kumar's question – "Why is this in *India Currents*?" – with implicit reference to these goals. It was a sensible, appropriate, and necessary question. But I always had the sense that it was not a question that mainstream outlets such as the *New York Times* or the *San Jose Mercury News* or *The Atlantic* needed to ask themselves – at least not in the same way.

The mainstream media had only to determine if a particular subject or story was *worthy* of being covered; the subject would then increase in value by virtue of selection and inclusion. The ethnic media, on the other hand, had to bend each story to its frame and create the ethnic angle that would not just warrant inclusion but also *permit* publication. In effect, the ethnic media had assigned itself a role as a supplement to the mainstream media, as opposed to a rival or counterpart. Thus, there was always a limit to the content any ethnic outlet had the right, obligation, and brief to produce.

"Why is this in *India Currents*?" Inevitably, this question would follow my introduction of topics that did not seem to be essentially "Indian American": poetry, social work, global warming, modern art. Invariably, I had to answer the question by profiling Indian poets and Indian social workers, or by asking Indian scientists and Indian artists to "share their journeys" with our readers. We had to make it *Indian* – if not by authorship then by interviewee – in order to publish it in *India Currents.* Our content was thus structurally and methodologically quite predictable, even when we were exploring new thematic grounds.

The irony, I swiftly found, was that many Indians and Indian Americans who *we* wanted to feature didn't necessarily want to be featured by *us.* Some turned down interview requests, perhaps for fear of seeming to relate only to an ethnic audience, for fear of being typecast later, or for fear of having to answer stock questions about their careers in relation to familial expectation and what it meant to be an ambassador for "the community." For example, celebrities such as the Indian American actress Mindy Kaling of *The Office* were very much on my editorial radar. It would have been terrific to publish a profile of Kaling, but it was impossible for a small, community outlet such as ours to score an interview with her. We tried and failed. So, instead, we featured Kaling in an end-of-year top-ten list of successful Indian Americans on television. Meanwhile, Kaling was interviewed by the likes of *Vanity Fair* and *Salon*, meeting those publications' criteria for diversity and inclusion, while benefiting herself from the mainstream exposure to a non-Indian (which is to say, non-community) audience.

A further irony: When Indian Americans such as Kaling were profiled in mainstream outlets, it was often their (exotic, inscrutable, groundbreaking, first-ever) Indianness that was emphasized.[15] Whereas coverage by an ethnic publication operating without the same diversity imperative could, in theory, be far more nuanced, individualized, and attuned to a wide range of imperatives beyond the burden of representation.

In any event, it was not surprising to me that famous Indians, aspiring celebrities, and icons with mainstream appeal resisted being hailed by our "community" magazine. They did so for the same reasons I initially resisted the community center story: to avoid being interpellated into a "we."

"We" is a method of inclusion. And sometimes, we don't want to be.

* * *

But, sometimes, we do.

The first thing I noticed when I began editing *India Currents* was how many of our regular freelance writers addressed a "we" in their articles. This, in turn, had varying effects on our readers. Readers who identified as Indian or South Asian were always faced with the choice of whether or not they wanted to be implicated in the narrative, argument, or anecdote in question. "Am I," they had to ask in response to every sentence read, "part of this 'we' or 'us' being deployed?" And to what end?

Meanwhile, those who identified as non-Indian, who read the magazine as a text representative of "an-other" culture, had to reconcile their own "otherness" to the shared assumptions, knowledges, and bilingual asides of an "imagined" and actual community of writers and readers.

Ethnic media outlets use "we" as a method of inclusion. They ask their readers to engage with the persistent deployment of ethnicity in the form of "we" and provide a forum within which different visions and versions of community might be complicated and challenged. This demands from readers a heightened level of investment, shared responsibility, and attention to potentially problematic representations of the community in question. At their best, ethnic media inaugurate new structures of accountability, foster what I have elsewhere termed "accented" reading practices, and lay claim to the enduring value of critical self-awareness.[16]

Certain letters that I received during my editorship indicated that *India Currents'* regular readers were engaged in precisely this kind of work: for example, a response from an Indian reader to our August 2008 cover story on yoga vacations in India. The story was written by Sarita Sarvate, an Indian American writer who had traveled to Kerala for a yoga retreat, only to find herself in a new age ashram populated primarily by white Americans and Europeans. Sarvate's article tried to come to grips with her conflicted feelings of belonging and entitlement and her experience of being a tourist among tourists in her "native" land. She described cringing when she heard *slokas* badly mispronounced in American accents, while she herself was unable to assume certain yoga positions.

The reader's Letter to the Editor criticized what she perceived to be Sarvate's hostility to non-Indians at the ashram, and it was almost conspiratorial. "I would advise," she wrote to me, "that we avoid creating misunderstandings between Indians and American readers."[17]

"We."

* * *

Fast forward a few years. I had gone back to school to pursue a PhD in the interdisciplinary humanities and was no longer editing *India Currents*. Still, I kept writing a regular column for the magazine and was generally keeping up with it. I began to notice that it was changing. There was something different about the stories being featured. The level of the prose felt to me less, well, professional. I set up a meeting with the then-editor and publisher. What was going on?

Over lunch the new editor shared with me her vision of what a community magazine needed to do and be: to literally give voice to the community. If anyone who identified as part of the community wrote an article, she said, it was the magazine's job to polish it up as well as possible and publish it.

This had not been my editorial philosophy. As editor, I had regularly been surprised by the fervor of *India Currents'* dedicated readership: from those longtime subscribers who wrote (even faxed!) Letters to the Editor, to those who phoned on a whim for restaurant recommendations, to those who regularly submitted unsolicited op-eds and feature stories. But I was also often annoyed by their neediness. Unlike the Mindy Kalings of our community, many readers felt entitled to coverage. If they couldn't get attention from the *New York Times*, then surely, they could get it from *India Currents*. Every single week of my two-year editorial tenure, I received emails and phone calls from parents of children who had won local contests, dancers who had performed in small festivals, and authors of self-published books that had been overlooked by mainstream reviewers. Members of the community presumed that *India Currents* would be interested in featuring them and expected inclusion in our pages. "I would like to be interviewed," they said, and were baffled when I weakly responded that we would give the matter "full consideration." I never let anyone down hard. I just didn't think it was our job to indiscriminately publish all their stories.

I had been operating under a different conception of what it meant to be a community outlet. When I was at the helm, the magazine was not a microphone or mirror for the community. Rather, the magazine as I envisioned it posed a representational *challenge* to the community. The magazine was of the community but apart; it operated on a different discursive register.

Under the new editorial dispensation, the space between the magazine and its readers was collapsing. The community was writing (for) itself.

I rejected this philosophy. But I see now the extent to which I had relied upon the investment and embrace of all those readers whose articles I'd declined to publish, whose children I hadn't featured, and whose stories went untold. I had depended upon those readers' "feelings" – their affective investments in identity, pride in roots and legacies, and desire for recognition and representation – as preexisting conditions of their engagement with the magazine, even as I chafed against their demands. I disdained the project of uncritically inculcating belonging, pride, and recognition in our readership. But I wouldn't have been able to do my job if that structure of feeling didn't already exist.

* * *

"We" is a method of inclusion – with implications that demand our uneasy grappling with certain questions. What if we write "we," but then bring it to crisis? What happens when we interpellate "we," but then take it for granted? Can we speak as "we," and then slowly expand our remit? Do we write toward "we," then tighten the circle?

To adapt Palumbo-Liu's words, the real question is not how to get beyond community, but rather *how to get to it* in the first place.

I struggled to "call it community" on day one. Now, I wonder: did I ever reach?

2

Of exclusion

> [The family] is, at root, the name we use for the fact that care is privatized in our society.
>
> Sophie Lewis[1]

In 2013, I became a mother.

In 2011, I became a wife and daughter-in-law.

In 1987, I became a sister.

In 1985, I became a daughter, granddaughter, niece, cousin.

I was born into a sphere of relation. We all are. Whether by volition or happenstance, each of our lives unfolds a serial process of becoming in terms of who we are and who we have been – not as individuals, but as subjects in relation to other people. Someone's friend. Someone's neighbor. Someone's child. Chief among these people are those whom we call *family*, whether immediate or extended, nuclear or chosen. This is not because familial relations are always more important, vital, or meaningful than other relations, but rather because of the privileged biological, legal, and social status of the family.

The family is the dominant mode of organizing human relationships the world over. In technical terms, this dominance is ideologically constructed. I am using the term "ideology" in the sense specified by Marxist cultural theorist Louis Althusser: as "the system of the ideas and representations which dominate the mind of a man or a social group," and on which the capitalist class depends for the maintenance of the social order.[2] As Althusser put it in his canonical essay on "Ideology and Ideological State

Apparatuses," "ideology represents the imaginary relationship of individuals to their real conditions of existence."[3] Ideology is not, in other words, an illusion of or about reality. It is not simply fantasy, mystification, or false-consciousness. It is not born of a failure to apprehend reality. Rather, ideology is an illusion of a relation to reality. Ideology is, fundamentally, *relational*. Ideology is a relation.

Althusser's key insight is that all individuals are interpellated by ideology as subjects. Indeed, we are all always already subjects practicing various rituals of ideological recognition and misrecognition. We are pre-appointed as subjects, even before we are born. Feminist theorists have extended these insights of Althusser's, in observing the workings of performative locutions that do the work of gendered subjection and ideological interpellation, such as "It's a girl!"[4] The interpellations with which this chapter begins – mother, daughter, wife, child – perform analogical work.

Over the course of our lives, we realize ourselves as subjected and, at the same time, we realize ourselves in subjection. This is what Althusser means when he writes that "subjects 'work by themselves'."[5] In Michel Foucault's equally iconic account, self-regulating subjects are bound "by the chain of their own ideas."[6] We are inhabitants of a society that functions at broad scale through the logic of the Panopticon, in which each individual has internalized the principle of surveillance, acts as if their actions are visible to power, and therefore conforms to regulatory norms. The words quoted in this paragraph are from Foucault's *Discipline and Punish: The Birth of the Prison*. But the reason his words have been so profoundly influential for multiple generations of scholars across fields is that this account far exceeds the specific position and institutional form of the prisoner and prison as such. In various ways, in multiple contexts, we each become "the principle of [our] own subjection."[7]

To stay with my own example, the sphere of relations known as *my family* has gradually expanded over the years: without my choice, as in the birth of my younger brother; and because I willed it, as in my decision to partner and get married. In the process, I have been and become routinely subjected to the workings of ideology regarding who I am in (illusory) relation to these others with whom I am (really) in relation. Over the first three decades of my life, I – like countless others – made a circular journey from given-inherited bio-family (parents) to chosen-legalized family (spouse) to given bio-family (children), binding myself anew in each life phase to the strictures of an institution from which I – like you – will never be liberated. Again and again, I keep choosing my own subjection to the family.

Do I want to? Do you? Can we say no to being interpellated by the family? What – let us ask the question anew – is the family?

The family is a social, cultural, legal, and economic institution that may be (but is not always) determined and organized by biological and genetic kinship ties or the accident of birth. To be part of a family is to belong to a collective that can speak and be spoken as a "we": that is, the "we" of *our* family. But, counter to the operations of the *inclusive* "we" discussed in Chapter 1, the "we" of the family I consider in this chapter functions primarily as a tool of *exclusion*. To put a finer point on it, to invoke the "we" of the family is fundamentally to perform an act, or institute a system, of enclosure, as opposed to extension or redistribution. Even the embrace of a friend as part of one's "chosen" family or the acknowledgment that someone is "like" family is a speech-act that rhetorically reinforces the privileged sphere of familial relation – the family proper, which requires no qualification. In Michèle Barrett and Mary McIntosh's words, "the family creates and recreates the very divisions it is often thought to ameliorate."[8]

* * *

Nowhere is the exclusivity of the family on display more clearly than in its conscription into the global project of neoliberalism – which is the form of family I discuss in what follows. As feminist philosopher Sophie Lewis puts it in *Abolish the Family*, neoliberalism appoints "kin, instead of society, responsible for the poor."[9] On this account, the family is the primary unit of capitalism, one that has been reduced, in Marx and Engels' words, "to a mere money relation."[10] It seems to operate on its own, for its own good, through rational self-interest, but it is in fact primarily serving to sustain labor power for capitalist exploitation. The family is, on the one hand, "a self-sufficient enterprise"; on the other hand, its chief task is to reproduce the working class.[11] The family is thus the most vital alibi of neoliberal states everywhere, which depend upon the family to do what should properly be the state's work: the work of education, healthcare, caretaking, housing, and social provision, broadly defined.

To be clear: what Lewis calls "family abolition" should not be confused with the violence of, for example, "family separation."[12] As feminist theorist Kathi Weeks points out, the nuclear family that we know to be a "white, settler, bourgeois, heterosexual and patriarchal institution" has also "served sub-ordinated groups as a fence against the state, society and capital."[13] The family serves, in other words, to both marginalize and protect. Faced with the organized abandonment of the neoliberal state, many marginalized, racialized, disenfranchised populations actually have nowhere to turn but their families. But that is also the point.

As numerous scholars have observed, the dismantling of the Anglo American welfare state starting in the mid-twentieth century required the maintenance of the unwaged provision of care within the family, particularly by women and mothers, even as those same caregivers were then also required to work as wage-laborers outside the home.[14] In *Family Values*, sociologist Melinda Cooper explains how this works: "[N]eoliberals are very much invested in the idea of 'family responsibility' – by which they mean the unpaid responsibility of private households to ensure risk, provide health care and pay for the education of children and the elderly. The difference between this and the family wage system of Fordism is that neoliberal States don't subsidize the delegation of 'welfare functions' to women via the male breadwinner wage."[15] In theory, family means *love*. In truth, family means *labor*. It is a restricted domain for the organization of work and the provisioning of care. For this reason, Lewis recounts, free universal childcare was at one point "a middle-of-the-road feminist demand." But, as the family has been further deformed by neoliberalism, this demand has not only been "defeated" but "actively erased."[16]

Take the US example. For most middle- and working-class families with care responsibilities for children or elders, it is not financially tenable for one adult or parent to be "stay-at-home." This is a "privilege" reserved for the upper-middle-classes and the wealthy, who routinely outsource the domestic labor of child-rearing, eldercare, and housekeeping to working-class women who, following Arlie Hochschild, then have "second" and third shifts of care work for their own families after their first shifts outside the home.[17] (This is also a global dynamic. Consider the international division of labor in which migrant women from Southeast Asia, for example, provide domestic and reproductive labor for families in Europe and the Middle East, while their own children, time zones away, are reared by others.)[18]

The "we" of the neoliberal family thus functions primarily as a method of guaranteeing debt repayment, apportioning inheritance, and delivering care in such a way as to specifically and hierarchically place the needs of the family above the needs of everyone else. The family serves "to replace welfare";[19] inheritance functions as a primary driver of wealth inequality.[20] This is true whether we are talking about the atomized unit of the "Western" nuclear family of four – heterosexual romantic parent-couple, two kids, a house, a dog, and a picket fence – or the larger unit of the "Eastern" intergenerational family, with an uncle in the bedroom upstairs, grandparents in the in-law unit, and cousins across the street. What is at issue, in other words, is not the size or scale of the family under capitalism but more fundamentally its nature: the fact that its "we" is "possessive"[21] and characterized by what Alexandra Kollontai called bourgeois "property love."[22]

In this way, the family ends up serving not just as an alibi for the state but also as a powerful alibi for political failure. In 2016, white American voters played the decisive role in delivering Donald Trump's first presidential victory. In the wake of his election, it became clear that white liberals' uninterrogated loyalty to their families had led to decades of avoidance of racism, fascism, white supremacist ideology, and misogyny – all because it was coming from within the family fold. Ignoring the sins of one's family amplifies the violence of erasure of all those "cast out as not kin."[23] White Americans, you must "lose your kin," Black studies scholar Christina Sharpe urged. What she was saying was "abolish the family."

* * *

On some level, we already know all this. We know that the family works through exclusion: by asking us to repeatedly choose its needs and demands over those of everyone and everything else. As I settle deeper into a decade-plus of parenthood, I am acutely aware of how being a mother has weakened (and in some cases, actively strained) my ties to others, simply by routing my time and energy in one particular direction. However community-minded one is, however politically active or socially committed, however outward-facing one's profession, family is a socially acceptable mode of exclusion, a method of prioritizing some over others, and an alibi for overinvestment in the well-being of a few people – the ones whom you can, proprietarily, call yours.

Every morning I wake up around 5:15 and pack my children's lunchboxes and two snacks each; sometimes, I also make their breakfast. Meanwhile, my partner wakes them up and supervises their tooth-brushing and dressing and backpack-packing. Then he walks the little one, our first grader, to school, while I clean up after their mess of leftover waffles and spilled milk. In the evenings, we drive the older one, our middle-schooler, to her swim team practices. We might quiz him on spelling bee words or check over her problem sets. Lunchboxes must be unpacked and cleaned for the next day. Dinner must be made and shared. We brush their hair and lotion their bodies; we fulfill the wishes on their Christmas lists. We schedule piano lessons for one and design science experiments with the other. We pick up phone calls from our children's schools (the rest can go to voicemail). We assume the risk of their exposure to viruses. We pay their bills and clear their debts, and one day we will leave them our assets: our house, our car, our bank accounts, whatever money we've squirreled away.

From the micro to the macro, the daily grind to the financial legacy: It's an extraordinary investment of time, labor, and resources. And it's extraordinarily, disproportionately focused on two individual children in a world of billions.

When I think about all the things I have done and will do for my two children, I am a little embarrassed. My children are no more or less deserving of love, care, or time than any other children, just as I am no more or less deserving than any other being on earth. At the same time, I admit that I am proud of being a version of what our society considers to be a good mother and responsible parent. I brought these two children into the world through my ("assisted")[24] reproductive labors, and so, it is my duty to extend to them all the care and love that I can – and I do. But there my responsibility officially stops in the eyes of American society. Nobody has ever asked me if I fed the child next door, although he may be starving. But if I starve my own children they will be removed from my "possession."

This is what Kollontai called "bourgeois morality": a morality that demands "all for the loved one" as opposed to "for the collective."[25] Likewise, for Raymond Williams, the problem is not human relations (not "we") but rather the bourgeois deformation of those relations (how "we" functions as a method of privatization).[26] Williams argued for a recognition of "working class culture" in which conceptions of familial obligation, care, and service might extend to all sectors of society, in contrast to the state of affairs in which each atomized family confronts other families in a competitive sphere. What makes the family exclusive, then, is that it is bound not only by relations of privacy and individualized responsibility but also by property logic. To this end, the family is a resource that some have and some hoard, while others are left bereft. At the same time, once you have a family, you can't easily get out of or away from it. There are few things as universally condemned as a parent's abandonment of their children, or an adult child's willful estrangement from ailing, destitute, or otherwise needy parents.

Critics of capitalism know that when we are in thrall to our possessions, when we are consumed by the culture of ownership, the result is that we get owned. Market logics dictate that one can never have enough or be enough.[27] Everything one does has to be instrumentalized and optimized. In much of the world, the family is the primary site of this optimization. Children are trained almost from birth to develop themselves as human capital, and parents are expected to invest in their children as if they are literal human resources who should be exploited in pursuit of the maximum return on investment. And why not? After making little Johnny a lifetime of breakfasts and lunches, is it too much to ask that he would make it onto the basketball team, score high on the SAT, and bring home a college scholarship?

In the present conjuncture, parents not only act as if they own their children but are given to assume responsibility for their children's successes or failures. If your child drops out of school, it is not society's fault – it is yours. As a result, and to stay with the above example, even if little Johnny's parents radicalize their approach to parenting, let go of their possessive investment in his performance, take a progressive approach to his childhood, and allow him to pursue what Avram Alpert terms "the good-enough life,"[28] little Johnny still has to live in a world filled with optimized, maximized resource-hoarders whose parents have overinvested in their potential in the name of securing *their* socioeconomic position in a hyper-competitive and radically unequal society. For Lewis, the project of "abolishing" the family thus has to begin by dismantling the idea that having a child is "an act of authorship [that] in turn generates, for the authors, property rights in 'their' progeny."[29]

To say that differently, the problem is not little Johnny's self-involved parents. The problem is the sociopolitical and economic context in which families are forced to function exclusively, as private firms. In *Hyper Education*, sociologist Pawan Dhingra illuminates another aspect of this story, building on seven years of research with American educators, parents, and students, especially from Asian American families.[30] For these families, Dhingra writes, the drive for enrichment education for their children (the SAT-prep classes and so on) is fundamentally a response to inequality: more specifically, it is a response to the existing inequities in educational systems that have historically been (and remain) spaces of white privilege and white normativity. Compared to Asian Americans and other minorities, white Americans hold disproportionate social and cultural capital; they are heirs to assets, networks, and the proverbial old boys' clubs. Asian Americans and other minorities try to match such capital by cultivating their own human and social capital as an alternative means of upward mobility.

This example lays bare the self-reinforcing nature of the family as a sphere of private solutions to public problems. In an unequal environment in which the cards are stacked against you, you have to look out for yourself and your own. But in doing so, in putting all your eggs into the basket of the family, you risk withdrawing further into the insular and atomized world of your own growth, development, safety, security, and success. Meanwhile, everyone around you is running on the same hamster wheel.

This is why Barrett and McIntosh characterize the family as a "trap" and a "prison" that is at base "anti-social."[31] The family, they write, "embodies the principles of selfishness, exclusion and pursuit of private interest and contravenes those of altruism, community and pursuit of the public good."[32] While it is of course true that family and community need not be mutually exclusive commitments, my point in highlighting these arguments is to emphasize the ways in which their respective "we's" function at cross-purposes. After all, it matters far less what is happening in the public schools if you come home to private tutors. And it doesn't matter at all how long the school bus will take to drop you home if you have someone on call to pick you up.

* * *

And so, we end up living not only *with* but also *for* our families. At the same time, we chafe against them. Daily, monthly, yearly, I find myself capitulating to the big and small demands of family: from responsibilities to my parents, to caretaking of my children, to obligatory visits to far-flung relations on four continents. I resent them. Still, I say yes. I love them. Still, I resist. I reject the overfamiliar assumptions of those who are adamant that because they knew me when, they know me now, and because they did for me then, I must do for them now.

Over the course of our lives, we variously disentangle ourselves from and entangle ourselves with our familial others. Sometimes, in their proximity, they are oddly estranging. Sometimes, when disavowed, they obstinately stick on. Through it all, what the persistence of the family fundamentally lays bare is the lie of individuality. We need others. We have always required care. There is comfort, security, and solace in knowing that there have been witnesses to our attempts at living. And who can deny that we accrue debts and obligations over the course of our lives, and that we do in fact owe something – maybe everything – to those without whose support we might never have lived at all?

The family remains a powerful sphere of attachment because it includes the people from and to whom many of us primarily receive and give love, care, and support of various kinds. It represents the only supposedly "non-contingent" guarantee we have of any of that.[33] This is why no less astute a critic of capitalism than Hochschild nevertheless refers to the family as "our most precious and emotionally powerful form of mutual commitment."[34] In Lewis's words, it is "the reason we are supposed to want to go to work, the reason we have to go to work, and the reason we *can* go to work."[35] Thus, as Barrett and McIntosh put it, cathecting to the family is a "highly rational choice given the material and ideological privilege accorded to it in our society."[36] By that same token, it is a choice that few people can afford not to make – which means it is not really a choice at all, but rather "blackmail passing itself off as fate."[37]

Beginning in spring 2020, the ravages of the Covid pandemic revealed the gross inadequacy of the family as a substitute for large-scale social welfare. Even some conservative commentators sought to renovate the family in light of Covid – while cannily preserving its exclusionary function. In a viral March 2020 essay, David Brooks questioned the dominance of the nuclear family form in the United States, calling it "a mistake." And yet, Brooks did not actually seek to change anything about how families work. Rather, in his vision, care would still be privatized among kin, whether given, chosen, or forged.[38] The "tables" would just be bigger, the family relations "thicken[ed] and broaden[ed]."

But more people – even refashioned as "family" – who are willing to pick up the pieces (and contribute to your emergency "Go Fund Me") does not an inclusive society make. Simply expanding from the scale of the nuclear family to that of the intergenerational family does not serve as an adequate corrective to the family's fundamentally exclusive operations.

We resist the family, we return to the family, and through it all the family disappoints and only minimally satisfies our needs, because it is designed to fail. This is Lewis's argument: Fundamentally, we want more from the family than it can, by definition, deliver. We want "reciprocal care, interdependence, and belonging." We want "cohabitation, collective eating, leisure, eldercare, and childrearing."[39] But true reciprocal care and interdependence would obliterate the mechanisms of exclusion that the "we" of the family creates.

There is no escaping the family. Some would argue it provides the blueprint for every other "we" we create and inhabit. But perhaps we might yet transform it, by transforming our conceptions of who we want to be to each other, of our desires and responsibilities.

In the name of the family – and, equally, against it – to whom might we ultimately belong?

3

Of communion

I have to be more and less than me to be truly with you.

R. Radhakrishnan[1]

Some years ago, I wrote a work of dialogical literary criticism with the scholar R. Radhakrishnan. It began as a co-written review of a co-written book called *Thinking Literature across Continents* by Ranjan Ghosh and J. Hillis Miller. It ended up offering a metacritical analysis of the very premise of thinking and writing together.

Radha (as friends call him) described our writing as a "*jugalbandi* – a duet [in Indian classical Hindustani or Carnatic music in which each artist] alternately take[s] the lead, playfully, competitively, entwined in our improvisations."[2] He wrote:

> I am responding to you, riffing off of you, and at the same time saying my own things, whatever that may mean. I am ethically concerned that what I say ought to, as a categorical imperative, be in response to your thoughts. In other words, I should do more than merely juxtapose my thoughts with yours. I have the obligation to achieve substantive intertextuality with your text; and at the same time, I should experience my freedom to indulge in my own thinking, but as a function of my differential and perhaps dialectical interaction with your insights . . . In this conversation with you (Mitsein and not just Dasein), I have to be more and less than me to be truly with you.[3]

In my response to Radha, I described what I in turn understood to be the nature of dialogue: It begins with relationality and at the same time produces relationality – both at once. Given true receptivity to the other's words, a dialogue that begins with recognition can then open up "a relation of contamination, mutual imbrication, involvement, and vulnerability."

Addressing Radha, I produced a response that was "both an absorption of and a reply to [his] text."[4] I wrote:

> "I have to be more and less than me to be truly with you," Radha writes. This, it seems to me, beautifully captures the aspiration of the dialogic: not only to encounter the other of and within the self... or the self in and of the other, but rather to move beyond relations of inclusion/exclusion and inside/outside toward practices of self-reinvention, reformation, and revision.
>
> Put differently... what a dialogue requires is the willingness to suspend the impulse for self-preservation... [C]ommunication, to say nothing of communion, requires that we not only not negate or neutralize each other, but that we actually give up our-selves. This giving up might firstly involve the acknowledgment that, in Donna Haraway's words, "we are not immediately present to ourselves." Then, an admission that my "belief" is never mine alone. Then, the realization that "I" have not the power to negate "you." Also, that if we are to be contemporaries (which is to say, contemporaneous with one another), I not only have to be more than and less than a self to be with you, but I also have to be before, with, and after you, with you at once in the past, present, and future of this exchange.[5]

Reading these words now, I am struck by the fact that Radha and my attempt to co-write a simple book review produced this philosophical exploration of the relationship between self and other. Our task had supposedly been to analyze Ghosh-Miller's efforts to think literature "across continents." But as we wrote to and with each other, we became consumed with analyzing the form and force of our jugalbandi.

Why did inhabiting a page together feel so profound? Was our writing always already relational, or did we produce our relation, word by word? How did our mutual address transform the possibilities for each of our own self-expression? In thinking about *Thinking* together, we demonstrated how "we" might be used as a method of communion.

* * *

Communion: "the interchange or sharing of thoughts or emotions; intimate communication; association; fellowship; the act of sharing something or holding it in common, or the state of something so held."

This chapter is about dialogical writing collaborations that produce communion: writing that starts with a practice of being "we" together on the page and ends up also enabling the expression of each writer's "I." Each literary exchange I discuss demonstrates what it means to be, in Radha's words, "both bound and liberated" by the "thoughts and contributions" of the one with and to whom one writes.[6] Each is an act of weaving and entanglement, a joining or "joy-ning" that enables vulnerability and revelation.[7]

I'm going to begin again counterintuitively, by discussing what will at first seem like a *single*-authored work – Jhumpa Lahiri's 2015 Italian memoir, *In Other Words* – but which, on closer scrutiny, reveals the extent to which even a stridently individual authorial "I" may be subtended by a network of relation. Then, I will turn to examples of poetic collaborations and consider what they reveal about the surprising affordances of "we."

In Other Words tells this story: In 2012, Lahiri, the Pulitzer Prize-winning, English-language fictionist, moved to Rome. There, she began a new phase of her artistic life in which she pledged to read and write only in Italian. Lahiri chose Italian because it was neither her parents' language (Bengali) nor that of her American peers (English). Italian was hers alone, and it was the first language in which she wrote from the perspective of her own "I."

Ironically, writing in Italian also meant that Lahiri could no longer write on her own. Despite her relative fluency in Italian, which she had studied on and off for years, writing *In Other Words* required the aid of "dictionaries, language teachers, editors, and friends"[8] who actively worked with Lahiri during the drafting, editing, and publication process.

Put simply, *In Other Words* registers a contradiction: The author's most deeply personal book about linguistic demolition and metamorphosis is also her most collaboratively written text.[9] As Lahiri notes in the book's acknowledgments, she could not have written in Italian without the essential scaffolding of others.[10] And yet, despite the significant supports undergirding her memoir's production, almost every sentence of the book is a declaration of Lahiri's autonomy: "I decide to move to Italy. I choose Rome"; "I renounce expertise to challenge myself. I trade certainty for uncertainty"; "[I] no longer feel bound to restore a lost country to my parents"; "On the page I am alone."[11]

Lahiri's account of her journey from English into Italian lays bare the twin desires I argue are at the heart of collaborative writing more generally: the desires to both write and unwrite the self. Lahiri started writing in Italian because she sought a new vantage from which to explore her *own* mind, artistic process, and preoccupations – not because she wanted to write about Italy or Italians. "I believe," she wrote, "that what can change our life is always outside of us."[12] Lahiri also chose to write in Italian because she did not "feel authoritative" in the language the way she did in English, and she wanted to learn "again, to write."[13] She sought the thrilling experience of not knowing and of not "belong[ing] completely" to the language.[14] She craved an experience of unbridgeable "distance"[15] from her own writing and, once again, from herself. Against the affordances of expertise, Lahiri sought ignorance, amateurism, the vertigo of learning to speak, an experience of walking on the moon – with all the inevitable stumbles she would take along the way. She wanted to defamiliarize and renew her "I." "It's not possible to become another writer," she reflected, "but it might be possible to become two."[16]

Let me state the obvious: The vast majority of writers cannot do what Lahiri did. Most of us do not have the reputation or resources to move across the world and remake ourselves as writers of some other language – nor, for that matter, would critics and publishers be particularly interested in just any writer's performance of amateurism. But many of us share Lahiri's desire to become "another writer" – to forge a new writerly persona, to start anew with nothing to lose and everything to gain, to experience afresh the joy of coming into one's own as an artist, maker, and thinker. What, then, is the regular old writer to do? The path open to the rest of us is dialogical collaboration: sustained, in-depth engagement with other writers as co-practitioners.

If you're a lab scientist or engineer, this might sound too obvious. Collaboration is a standard mode of knowledge production in the sciences and even social sciences, after all. But it has long been undervalued in the humanities. In my own academic field of literary studies, promotion remains contingent upon the publication of single-authored monographs. Co-authored work doesn't quite count, and therefore it doesn't happen very often. The irony is that collaborative writing is incredibly hard to pull off and can be very rewarding. This is something literature scholars are only just starting to recognize – and also why my jugalbandi with Radha was so special.[17]

What academics are just learning, poets have long known. As the co-editors of a volume on collaborative writing ask, "Why would a writer abandon their own particular voice for a mutant expression they can't quite control? Perhaps the allure lies in the challenge of having a puzzle to solve. Or a conundrum to cause. A contest. A love fest."[18] Undertaken seriously, with integrity and curiosity, collaborative writing is an opportunity to inhabit the voice-mind of another. It is a method of connection that enables the simultaneous emergence and disintegration of the self. In Natalie Diaz's words, addressed to Ada Limón in their poetic collaboration "Envelopes of Air," "This is my knee, since she touches me there. / This is my *throat*, as defined by her reaching. / I am touched – I *am*."[19]

In what follows, I discuss Diaz and Limón's exchange alongside two other poetic collaborations in which writers are "untethered and tethered all at once”[20] – from themselves as well as from each other. Taken together, they confirm what Frantz Fanon once described as the fundamental relationality of language: “To speak is to exist absolutely for the other.”[21] At the same time, they demonstrate how communion with the other – writing as “we” – might also enable a profound renovation and revelation of the self.

* * *

In 2011, Ross Gay and Aimee Nezhukumatathil began a correspondence that would become *Lace and Pyrite: Letters from Two Gardens.*[22] This chapbook of epistolary poems is divided into seasons and unfolds as a record of a year of “tending” to their respective gardens in Bloomington, Indiana and Fredonia, New York, as well as to “ourselves, our relationships, our earth.” The chapbook’s 12 poems are untitled and alternate between authors; each poem directly responds to the one that precedes it. “It’s exhausting, this desire,” Nezhukumatathil writes. “But I would never trade it for any shiny marble. Would you?” Gay’s response-poem hears the question and takes it up: “It’s true. No golden marble ” As Anissa Wardi puts it, the epistolary form of the poems “creates fluidity as the voices of the poet-gardeners layer and build upon one another, creating a kaleidoscopic reflection of the living world. Calling and responding to one another about gardens, loss, and love, the poets weave together a collection, an offering of elegiac joy.”[23] Each subtle textual movement underscores the poststructural insight that every utterance emerges into an existent context; the poet is never not replying to something that has been heard, seen, or encountered before. Each voice sounds only in and as a response to the other. Jugalbandi, again.

Although they do not carry explicit salutations (no “dear Ross” or “dear Amy”), many of the poems address an interlocutor through the second person. In the final poem of the “Winter” sequence, Gay does this to broach the issue of climate change. He hails his addressee – Nezhukumatathil, specifically, and the reader, generally – in order to communicate his individual experience of a collective crisis. "The earth is heating up, I mean to say. / Nothing like peach blossoms in February to tell you / something's off – when these / shivered and shimmied in the wind, / it was a full month early. / Do you know what I'm asking?" As the poem draws to a close, the speaker adds, "What am I trying to say?"

A more conventional poetic operation might have been to invite the reader along to see what the poet sees. Gay's questions instead invite the reader to respond to and think about the earth the way he does – even more, to think as him. "Thinking with" is at stake here, not thinking for, nor rendering present. The poet is not simply picturing his garden; in fact, this writing is not a representational project at all. Rather, the poet invites the reader to tend the garden with him, to inhabit a shared space-time of tending – and to share it with his friend.

As the poems continue, Gay and Nezhukumatathil begin to address each other more frequently: "You thought I said"; "Maybe you're right"; "You are on your own." On the one hand, this direct address serves to emphasize the fact of the book's having two distinct speakers who are in conversation. On the other hand, as the poets address each other more explicitly, they also inhabit each other's positions more fully: "I saw those ants too"; "You must know..."; "you'll remember..." Finally, writing to each other becomes a mode of communion, of writing toward a shared position of enunciation: "we." "[L]et us stop explaining," Gay writes. The final lines of the chapbook reference "us" as well: "The galaxy turning all around us / Turning us all around."

Despite their ultimate turn toward the collective – "us" – Gay and Nezhukumatathil sign each of their respective poems with their initials. But there are instances of collaborative writing in which individual authorship is more explicitly refuted. For example, every poem in Rushi Vyas and Rajiv Mohabir's "poetic conversation,"[24] *Between Us, Not Half a Saint*, is presented without attribution.[25] The "who-ness did not feel as important to the book itself," Mohabir has said. At the same time, each of the poets' first names occasionally appears in a poem, preserving both the fact and suggestion of direct address and single authorship.

Between Us offers a response to the "growing fanaticism" in/of the United States in the time of Trump and India in the time of Narendra Modi. Before starting to write their chapbook, Vyas and Mohabir agreed upon a series of rules, constraints, and challenges, such as: derive the syllabic structure of the poem from a Hindu mantra and "include at least one line/phrase/sentence" from a contemporary text (the resulting references range from Modi's 2019 acceptance speech to an NPR article about a dwindling bird population). In "Gayatri," the poet asks, "what grief / comes to a country that sees / oneness everywhere?"[26] In "Soca," the poet writes: "we both will soon be ashes. / How's this for unity?"[27] Questions of collectivity are fundamental to their project, with the implied hope that collaborative writing might produce a better response to creeping fascism than individual protest or lament.

Or, at least better writing. I want to circle back now to "Envelopes of Air" by Diaz and Limón, which consists of eight poems alternating between the authors as they explore the subjects of life, time, home, identity, and relation, as well as "the kinship of words and of being women." In a joint interview, the poets describe the experience of writing the poem-letters as one of "holding hands."[28] Already friends before they started writing together, the poets' relationship served as the foundation of their exchange. As they wrote, they tried to preserve the autonomy and distinction of their poem-letters. Thus, although they had an existing, routine correspondence consisting of emails, phone calls, and text messages, they never discussed the poem-letters while they were writing them. They sent the poem-letters to each other as email attachments, without disclaimer, so that they could inhabit a space outside of everyday communicative exchange. Additionally, Diaz and Limón never discussed bringing their exchange to a close. It was important to maintain the dream that they might go on writing poem-letters to each other forever. It was essential to the form that it was potentially endless.

The poems of "Envelopes of Air" are suffused with desire: desire to be heard, to connect, and to communicate. "I wish I could write to you from underwater," Limón writes.[29] ". . . all I want to do is tell you a story . . . / . . . I want to write / of the body as desirous, reedy, fine on the tongue . . ."[30] Each poet seeks to know who she herself is, but the question "who am I" can only be answered by the other: "Am I braver than those birds?"[31] At the same time, knowledge of the self is ironized as an impossibility, given the generations of obfuscation, forgetting, amnesia, and erasure that attend our joint inhabitance of this earth. "We know nothing / about ourselves," Diaz writes. And, in a later poem, "How is it that we know what we are?" It is a question that Limón will eventually send back to Diaz, in an echo of her voice.[32]

"Envelopes of Air" emphasizes embodied relationality. The poets exist for each other not only in time but *as* time, as a living archive of the temporal. Appropriately, one image that repeats throughout the poems is that of a train with no point of origin, a train that is always already in motion, a train that carries passengers who are both speakers and receivers. Limón writes: "I am always in too many worlds, sand sifting through my hands, / another me speeding through the air, another me waving / from a train window watching you / waving from a train window watching me." The bounds of outside and inside meet at the train window; the poet who looks is also the poet who is seen; the poet who waves is also the poet at whom one waves.

As they created the time-space of "Envelopes of Air," Diaz and Limón came to know each other, each other's lives and partners, and each other's literary craft much more deeply than they had before. They already shared the experience of being brown women writer-sisters, or "hermanas."[33] Thus, much that would have needed to have been translated and explained to other readers could go unsaid and between the lines. As in *Lace and Pyrite*, the epistolary form enabled the poets to circumvent the demands of realist representation, since the first addressee was already conversant with the psychic and territorial landscapes in question. Each poet trusted that the words she'd written would be received with love by someone whose words and world she in turn respected and loved. Each poet received the words of the other as a gift. The result was the most "authentic" poems either of them had ever written – and the most intimate poems either of them had ever read.

* * *

They say the age of letter-writing is over, that both the physical form of the letter (a piece of paper, folded, in a stamped and addressed envelope) and the materiality of the writing in question (by hand, in cursive, in ink) are lost arts.[34] But consider the work of Gay and Nezhukumatathil, Vyas and Mohabir, and Diaz and Limón. We are still living in a profoundly epistolary age, one in which technology, at its best, can be harnessed in service of deeper dialogues, collaborations, and writerly communion.

For years, many of us conducted our daily work and lives on email. And although email now seems to be going the way of the dodo bird and the telephone call, some of us are still carrying out lengthy correspondences with virtual pen friends. We address ourselves to others in text constantly. Scores of SMS, WhatsApp, and iMessage threads track our mundane and weighty back-and-forths with intimates and relative strangers alike: all those with whom – thanks to the ease of picking up a dormant thread – we are always already in conversation. Of course, a letter is not exactly the same as an email, which is not strictly equivalent to a text message relay, which is precisely not a rule-based poetic collaboration. But, in theory, all of these are forms of exchange, of *speaking to*, as opposed to simply speaking. They are modes of dialogical *address*, as opposed to modes of alienated, monologic expression such as, to anticipate the next chapter, posting status updates on X or TikTok videos into the virtual void.

Collaborative writing as "we" demands the deauthorization of the self in the name of exploration, artistic adventure, and intellectual risk. It's no easy feat. But in the process, the writer may be rewarded with a new conception of the self. In poet Divya Victor's words, collaboration is "one way of not remaining strangers"[35] – to each other, yes, but also crucially to ourselves, as we become more and less than the "I" we might otherwise have been.

What more might collaborative writing make possible – for us, for "we"?

How else might we learn to write together, in this increasingly strange, estranging, and isolating world?

4

Of isolation

> [D]igital communication has made community – the we – deteriorate markedly . . . heightening human isolation.
>
> Byung-Chul Han[1]

> We believe in the future of connection in the metaverse.
>
> Mark Zuckerberg[2]

Once upon a time, at the start of the twenty-first century, there was a widely shared dream that the internet would save us from ourselves. Social media platforms such as Facebook would enhance human connection, communication, and community. In the early 2010s, Twitter was held up as proof of the internet's democratizing tendencies, as it enabled revolutionary movements such as Occupy Wall Street and the Arab Spring.[3] As Jonathan Haidt puts it, recalling the optimism of the time, "What dictator could impose his will on an interconnected citizenry? What regime could build a wall to keep out the internet?"[4] I took a college class on internet policy, circa 2005, and I still recall my professor Kenneth S. Rogerson's indefatigable enthusiasm about "the long tail" of cultural production we were all poised to enjoy and his exuberant account of the new possibilities for robust civic engagement in the digital public square.[5]

That all feels rather quixotic today. Social media, we now know, is just as often "antisocial."[6] In the post-truth era of rampant mis- and disinformation, deepfake videos, and fake news spread by AI chatbots, as internet titans such as Elon Musk and

Mark Zuckerberg flagrantly refuse to moderate content on X and Instagram, it is clear how easily the relatively unregulated infrastructure of the internet was seized by monied corporations, global media tycoons, and bad actors seeking to maximize clicks, likes, retweets, and shares – all with the alibi of maximizing human connection. When Facebook hit two billion users in 2017, founder Zuckerberg emphasized exactly that commitment: "We're making progress connecting the world, and now let's bring the world closer together."[7] In 2021, Facebook, Inc. rebranded as Meta Platforms, Inc. with the tagline, "We believe in the future of connection in the metaverse."

Whatever Meta's official goal, it has been clear for years that, rather than connect people, digital communication is serving to fragment, atomize, and polarize: if not "destroying the public sphere and heightening human isolation," as philosopher Byung-Chul Han puts it, then certainly exacerbating existing tendencies toward loneliness, solitariness, and social anomie, especially among the younger generations of digital natives.[8] Rates of depression and anxiety that were stable in the 2000s rose dramatically after the advent of the smartphone. Suicide rates for adolescents, especially girls, have been rising by percentage points in the double and triple digits. The evidence is overwhelming. As psychology professor Jean M. Twenge writes: "All screen activities are linked to less happiness, and all nonscreen activities are linked to more happiness. All screen activities are linked to more loneliness, and nonscreen activities are linked to less loneliness."[9]

* * *

This chapter is about the deep irony at the heart of new communications technologies: the fact that they produce a "we" that confirms our apartness from others, not our togetherness, and heighten our detachment from the world, not our connection to it. In Judith Butler's words, we human beings "suffer from the condition of being addressable" – which is why we long for the kinds of dialogue, collaboration, and communion discussed in Chapter 3. Social media and digital communication "exploit all the ways that

[we] are present"; they exploit our "alertness . . . openness, and . . . desire to engage,"[10] using our human need for connection against us.

Etymologically, connection means "fastening together"; to be connected is to be "bound" or "tied." Being "connected" through digital media, by contrast, just means that you have access to individuals, information, and ideas to whom and with which you must still strive to build a relation. You can fly over the oceans with a laptop in tow, and when you land halfway across the earth, the world as figured by websites bookmarked will look exactly the same as it did wherever you came from. So, to whom or what, exactly, are you connecting? (Meanwhile, the seemingly ubiquitous worldwide network continues to exclude millions who remain on the other side of the digital divide. The more connected "everyone" is online, the deeper the disconnect from "everyone else" who isn't.)

Every day I wake up and reach for my phone, unless I've had the good sense to leave it in another room – which I generally don't. I connect to the internet. I connect to my email. I connect to the handful of sites from which I get the news. On one level, I am more *connected* to other people than would have been possible at any other time in history. In the time it takes me to type this sentence, I can also text my grandmother in Delhi and email my son's teacher in Houston and check the score in an Olympics game going on in Paris.

On another level, however, connectivity has never felt so prescribed and limited. Last year, I chaperoned a fifth-grade dance at the elementary school. There wasn't much dancing going on, and I spent most of the evening clearing girls out of the bathroom, where they were taking selfies and posting videos to TikTok. Meanwhile, my own smartphone sat in my purse racking up notifications on WhatsApp threads, most of them video forwards I would ultimately ignore. All of this – the TikToks, the text messages, "the constant multichannel communications with multiple audiences"[11] – is supposed to make us feel connected to one other. But does it? I use a smartphone that, as Han writes, promises me the liberation of total knowledge and easy access to information but "radiates a fatal compulsion – the compulsion to communicate."[12]

We have traded real connection for possible exchange, a kind of existential poverty with the illusion of abundance, a "potential for almost instantaneous contact [that] gives an encouraging feeling of already being together."[13]

Except that, in most cases, we are not. We are plugged in yet alienated at the same time. And "we" ends up serving as a method of isolation.

* * *

I recognize this sounds curmudgeonly and technophobic. But just pass by a line of students silently waiting for a school bus – each glued to a phone screen, ignoring everyone else – and you'll see what I mean. Or enter any university classroom five minutes before the bell rings. The students sit at their desks silently, looking at their phones. They aren't sharing notes or discussing the readings; they aren't even talking about what they did last night. They're doomscrolling, or texting someone in a different time zone, swiping left on a potential date who's not up to snuff, or else "phubbing" (phone-snubbing) the odd classmate who does try to initiate real-world, real-time conversation.[14] These observations are shared by numerous educators. In school principal Russell Shaw's words, observing how phones took over his high school's central meeting space: It "brings to mind a beetle infestation in a forest. At first, just one or two trees show signs of damage. Then, the next thing you know, the forest is a less healthy, less vibrant place than it once was."[15]

Smartphones, social media, and digital technologies more generally are all part of the infestation, all contributors to what Nate Holdren aptly describes as our contemporary "broken sociality."[16] And as with any sociological phenomenon, what's happening is happening on both micro and macro scales that then cross-pollinate. On the micro scale: alienation, "egoization," and "narcissification" of the individual subject. On the macro scale: political fragmentation, polarization, and the "atomization" of society as we know it.[17]

In his 2000 book *Bowling Alone: The Collapse and Revival of American Community* and the 1995 article that preceded it, political scientist Robert Putnam presciently diagnosed the threat that increasing isolation at the micro level would pose to American democracy at the macro level. Distinguishing between "bonding social capital" between alike individuals and "bridging social capital" across demographic difference, and using examples such as declining participation in bowling leagues, unions, and school PTAs, Putnam argued that "life is easier in a community blessed with a substantial stock of social capital." He wrote:

> In the first place, networks of civic engagement foster sturdy norms of generalized reciprocity and encourage the emergence of social trust . . . At the same time, networks of civic engagement embody past success at collaboration, which can serve as a cultural template for future collaboration. Finally, dense networks of interaction probably broaden the participants' sense of self, developing the "I" into the "we."[18]

Twenty-five years later, the networks of interaction and reciprocity that Putnam deemed crucial to democracy are weaker than ever. Interviewing Putnam in July 2024, Lulu Garcia-Navarro observed that "when it comes to social connection, things feel bad right now." Putnam concurred: "We've become more socially isolated, and we can see it in every facet of our lives."[19] In 1995, Putnam hypothesized that the "the technological transformation of leisure" by the advent of the television was partially to blame for our aloneness. It is now undeniable that new leisure and communications technologies – from Netflix to generative AI companions – are playing a huge part in our increasing isolation. As Haidt says, "[It's] obvious. It's common sense. Most people see it."[20]

The internet and social media have produced a collective subject that Han calls "the digital swarm." What distinguishes the swarm from other collectives (like, for example, the crowd, or, for that matter, the union) is that "no *soul* – no *spirit* – dwells within it. The soul gathers and unites. In contrast, the digital swarm comprises isolated individuals ... Individuals who come together as a swarm do not develop a *we*."[21] The swarm, in Han's estimation, lacks "the *interiority of assembly* that would bring forth a *we*. They form a *gathering without assembly – a crowd without interiority*."[22] Han draws an instructive contrast with radio as a technology that historically brought people together: for example, in anticolonial resistance movements.[23] Digital media, by contrast, are fundamentally productive of "solitude," not "solidarity."[24]

Phenomenologically speaking, there is limited presence in digital spaces like chatrooms and social media forums: no returned gaze, no repertoire of embodied gestures, no possibility of real interlocution. I receive a slew of text messages but hear no voice. I meet with a student virtually but can't actually look into his eyes. It turns out, as Putnam warned, that meeting in a Zoom room is not the same as meeting in a classroom.[25] Instead, we are each relegated to a corner of Narcissus's pool, where we await emoji affirmations as we stare, bizarrely, at our own faces, leading to psychological complexes such as "nomophobia" (fear of being without a mobile phone) and "Zoom dysmorphia."[26] As a result, Sherry Turkle writes, we are "alone together"; "we are forever elsewhere."[27]

At stake is the political itself – a fact that numerous researchers have recently taken up in work on social media as a technology of polarization that shapes political tribalism.[28] In Haidt's words, the rise of social media has "unwittingly dissolved the mortar of trust, belief in institutions, and shared stories that had held a large and diverse secular democracy together." Now, he writes, "we are disoriented, unable to speak the same language or recognize the same truth. We are cut off from one another and from the past."[29] This research builds on Putnam's predictions in *Bowling Alone*, as well as Cass Sunstein's prescient 2001 hypothesis in *Republic.com* that the internet would produce echo chambers, in which most people hear only the equivalent of their "own" voice.[30] As a result, we are seeing the resurgence of ethnonationalisms, globally, and the fracturing of the democratic consensus in the United

States, specifically.

To put a finer point on it, the social isolation that has long been observed among video-gamers and the cell phone-obsessed is a sign of a much more dangerous collective susceptibility to authoritarianism and fascism – a harbinger, even, of the decline of democracy. As I write these words, we are days away from the second presidential inauguration of Donald Trump. The world's richest man, Musk, daily blasts misinformation, disinformation, and "anti-regulation, anti-immigrant, anti-transgender, anti-press" screeds to over 20 million followers on X.[31] Zuckerberg's Meta has just announced that it will host "entertaining and engaging" AI "characters" on its social media platforms, who will have accounts just like regular users. [32] Thanks to the quick work of journalists, we already know that these characters are spewing racist "digital slop" that is "reinforcing cultural biases and stereotypes."[33]

The question is, what exactly are any of us going to do about it?

* * *

At an individual level, it's hard not to feel helpless about changing the way we interact with social media and the internet more generally, even for those of us who want to loosen its grip on our lives. For the teenagers filmmaker Lauren Greenfield followed in the docuseries *Social Studies*, social media is "inescapable"; opting out "threatens social death."[34] Although most parents know that their school-age children shouldn't be spending hours on their phones, the majority give in and let them because, as Ezra Klein notes, "eh, the other kids do."[35] As with climate change, as with the unchecked Covid pandemic, it is hard for isolated, atomized individuals to believe that their actions will make a meaningful difference to a larger social crisis.

What we need is collective action – which is finally, at the time of this writing, getting underway.

For example, studies have shown for years that cell phones have no place in education. They're responsible for "distracting students, isolating them, and creating unhealthy echo chambers that undermine critical thinking,"[36] while also encouraging cyberbullying and facilitating the orchestration of in-person violence. At long last, schools around the world have started banning them outright.[37] In July 2024, Virginia Governor Glenn Youngkin issued an executive order establishing "cell phone-free education" in K-12 public schools, in the name of physical health, mental health, and educational outcomes.[38] In November 2024, Australia banned social media use by all children under the age of 16.[39]

Such moves are encouraging and should bolster our individual efforts. I'll give my own example. I have two children, ages 12 and 7. My big kid would like a phone, but she doesn't have one, and she's not getting one. She's not getting one because I want to protect her labor, her time, her privacy, and her capacity to connect with other people. She's not getting one because I want to preserve her capacity for "deep attention."[40] She's not getting one because her primary task as a young person coming into her own is to develop a healthy sense of herself and her relationships to others – of both "I" and "we" – and smartphones and social media work against both.

I say this as a philosophical neo-Luddite as well as from experience. Like many of my generation, I joined Facebook in college, as soon as the site opened up to students outside Harvard. It was fun, at first. I got off the platform a few years later, when I began to feel more like a voyeur than a participant. I joined Twitter in 2015 and deleted my account in 2023 after Musk took over. I used it to follow journalists and academics, and was otherwise never particularly active. Before that, I was briefly on Instagram. I left that platform in 2013, just after the *Oxford English Dictionary* chose "selfie" as the word of the year. My big kid was a baby then, and I didn't want to participate in the intrusive cataloging and exhibition of her adventures in banana-eating and hand-clapping. At just a few months of age, she was already being seen, followed, shared, and commented on. I pressed delete before I could give up the story of her life to an algorithm.

With each deleted account, I knew I was choosing to forego something: easy "connections" with extended family; reminders to ping old school friends on their birthdays; videos of distant and close contacts that I would otherwise never see; a convenient venue for self-promotion. These were sacrifices I was willing to make. For too long, I had been privy to images and words that I actually didn't need to view, and which made me feel I knew their posters better than I did. The expectation that I in turn present myself to others via photos, article recommendations, and status updates had also become intolerable. Raised, like many women, to put other people's needs, opinions, and desires above my own, and trained, like many Asians, to always consider first what other people might say, social media reinforced exactly those tendencies that I was trying hard as an adult to unlearn.

To enlist a different vocabulary, social media demanded forms of affective labor that I was no longer willing to perform. In their research on this, sociologists Sophie Bishop and Brooke Erin Duffy show that rather than flatten hierarchies through venues for anonymous expression, the internet has instead entrenched gendered inequalities through the creation of new forms of devalued "women's work," including "memory work on behalf of friends and family, the coordination of events, and the provision of access to news and information."[41] Bishop and Duffy show that labor on social media is feminized in four distinct ways: through demands for emotional expression, the "discipline of aesthetics" through visibility, the imperative of being "always-on" (that is, available 24/7), and the broader dictates of consumer capitalism.[42] In addition, constant mobile connectivity – from phones on bedside tables and Alexa/Siri at the dinner table, to menstrual-cycle and fertility-tracking apps, to the perpetual harvesting of our location data – means that many people live without any privacy. Non-normatively gendered subjects in particular are heavily surveilled.

Of course, some users and posters do get paid for this access. The algorithms driving digital platforms reward performativity and the pursuit of virality, and there are many people who have happily ridden their Instagrams, TikToks, and YouTube channels all the way to the bank. As Duffy explains, "social media labor" has successfully been recast by tech companies as "monetizable leisure,"[43] and a new generation of aspiring "influencers" has been conditioned to accept and even invite intrusions into their privacy, as they perform for fans around the world.[44] Today, there are young children narrating their lives to online followers, who observe their every move from the remove of a cell phone screen. Ultimately, though, even the most successful influencers serve at the pleasure of the algorithm; they can never stop producing content or else they risk irrelevance.

Meanwhile, our personal data and immaterial labor are being monetized by corporations such as Meta, Alphabet, and Apple. Minute by minute, we are packaged and sold to advertisers, with the consequence that our physical and virtual worlds are saturated with more ads and increasing demands for our attention. Borrowing a term from the petrochemical industry, historian D. Graham Burnett observes that our minds are being "fracked":

> We have a, depending on who you ask, $500 billion, $3 trillion, $7 trillion industry, which, to get the money value of our attention out of us, is continuously pumping into our faces high-pressure, high-value detergent in the form of social media and non-stop content that holds us on our devices. And that pumping brings to the surface that spume, that foam of our attention, which can be aggregated and sold off to the highest bidder.[45]

We are being sold. At the same time, as Turkle argues, we are paying for the privilege of being fracked with our "empathic capacity." "Technology enchants," she writes. "It makes us forget what we know about life."[46] Instead of conversation, we have control over when we respond to texts. Instead of paying attention to our friends, we distractedly engage them while multitasking. Instead of focusing on meaningful activities, we learn to function with constant interruptions. "[W]e are more severed from each other now than at any time in human history," Burnett notes, "even as we have this kind of ersatz experience of our being aggregated in new and powerful ways."[47]

Even as I type these words, I am struggling to resist the urge to click over to the next screen to see if an email has arrived, or to read the news headlines, for the *n*th time this hour. Why? Because I have been habituated into the economy of distraction. I am bodily attuned to the accelerated experience of what Manuel Castells famously called "timeless time."[48] I am used to being everywhere and everytime talking to everyone doing everything all in an instant thanks to the machine. The machine that wants me to keep using it, as Turkle reminds us: "That is how they can get more data from you in order to sell more to you and others. Machines keep us in a world of machines."[49]

No wonder that there's a program that blocks websites, apps, and the internet so that we can be more present to ourselves, the people around us, and our work. Its name? *Freedom*.

* * *

The digital world serves up an illusory "we." Its simulacrum of connectivity disappears with the click of an *x* at the top of a screen. By that same token, it is here to stay. And I know what my critics will say: that old technologies were new once, too.[50] That a different generation thought the television spelled doom. That, in the polemical words of Michael Shellenberger and Ted Nordhaus, "[t]he solution to the unintended consequences of modernity is, and has always been, more modernity – just as the solution to the unintended consequences of our technologies has always been more technology."[51]

Sociologist Christopher Bail makes a version of this point: "In an era of growing social isolation, social media platforms have become one of the most important tools we use to understand ourselves – and each other."[52] Cautioning against technologically determinist theories of social problems (and for that matter, moral panics), Judy Wajcman encourages our attention to the affordances of digital media as it arrives into existing social, political, and economic contexts. Critiquing what she reads as the knee-jerk privileging of face-to-face communication over mediated communication, Wajcman questions the boundary between real and virtual communication and considers how digital media also serves to increase intimacy and reduce isolation.[53]

To be sure, all of us who lived through the Covid pandemic know that technology is a pharmakon: not just a poison, but also a cure. In the early months of social distancing, when the pandemic made nearby people feel far away, digital communication technologies brought far-away people close. We gathered online for Zoom birthdays and happy hours, virtual piano lessons, chess games, and online school. People met their soulmates online; they collaborated on books and art projects. Remote work enabled countless people to keep their health without losing their jobs.

I don't deny any of this. But just as, following Wajcman, we should not be technological determinists in our outlook, we should not, pace Shellenberger and Nordhaus, be technological solutionists, either. If we humans cannot connect with each other, there is little reason to believe that AI chatbots will be "facilitators of the human contact that the network has taken away."[54] Just because online school was a life-saving option in pandemic times, it doesn't mean Khan Academy videos should replace the synchronous, real-time environment of in-person school. Just because you can text with a friend, it doesn't mean you never need to see them. And just because people all over the world have access to the same information, it doesn't mean they have the same opportunities to use it – doesn't mean social media is "contributing to more equal lives and worlds."[55]

For sociologist Allison Pugh, the present moment in human history is one in which we are waging "a battle for our souls." Will technology exacerbate the "depersonalization crisis," our "loneliness and our social losses," or will it enable us to "prioritize connection" in new ways?[56] Will we learn to use digital communications for the benefit of everyday people – or will everyday people be used for the benefit of some corporate bottom line?

The task, as novelist Zadie Smith puts it, is to get beyond "the misguided belief that self-selecting, yet algorithmically determined, online communities are any decent political substitute for geographic, localized, politically diverse, real-world communities." We have to recognize that the truly "powerful and dangerous" political actors today are "tech bros" – and that they have built their empires on *our* attention, something we still have the power to withhold.[57]

Will we use that power? What actually deserves our attention – and who?

Writer Teju Cole frames the questions like this: “Does being with one’s people mean the possibility of traveling to see them? Does it mean having them living across town or next door? Does it mean phone calls, text messages, videoconferencing?”

How should we connect with those people with whom we “would wish to build a life”? Where will we find them – our people, “in whose presence” we might finally feel that “yes, this is life”?[58]

5

Of coercion

> Let's remember that we are all in this together. (May 13, 2021)
>
> We have the tools. (September 9, 2021)
>
> Joe Biden[1]

In 2022, the editors of the *Merriam-Webster Dictionary* surveyed Google searches and the newspapers of record and chose "gaslighting" as the word of the year. Distinguishing the practice of gaslighting from other forms of deception, such as "lying" and "fraud," they noted that gaslighting is at once personal, political, structural, and institutional; it can happen between individuals as well as on a broader social scale. They defined gaslighting as "the act or practice of grossly misleading someone especially for one's own advantage."[2]

This chapter responds to a specific species of gaslighting that unfolded in very recent history – indeed, that is unfolding still – and which was premised on the widescale misleading utilization of "we." "*We are all in this together.*" "*We have the tools.*" The epigraphs attribute these locutions to US President Joe Biden, speaking in 2021, but both of these statements were voiced by scores of others over multiple years, from journalists and policymakers, to preschool principals and factory owners, to the directors of the Centers for Disease Control (CDC) and World Health Organization (WHO).

The first – "We are all in this together" – was a widely articulated sentiment in the early months of 2020, when the Covid pandemic began to take hold globally. It was briefly empirical, then aspirational, then delusional, before becoming entirely coercive. A period of genuinely unprecedented fellow feeling and togetherness in the first couple pandemic months swiftly gave way to the mass disillusionment, anomie, and fragmentation that historian Nate Holdren, quoted in Chapter 4, has termed our "broken sociality."[3]

The second refrain – "We have the tools" – gained rhetorical force in 2021 and persists at the time of this writing. It served from the get-go as an alibi for a devastating series of rollbacks of pandemic policies and mandates, in the United States and around the world. With the advent of (unequally available) coronavirus vaccines and monoclonal antibodies, pharmaceutical interventions swiftly became the sole pandemic protection touted by the US government. These "tools" – which only some of us have – were used as a pretext to roll back masking, testing, vaccination, and quarantine requirements, before ultimately becoming a new source of profit extraction for the pharmaceutical industry.[4]

Taken together, these two locutions were the pillars of the shockingly successful gaslighting campaign that was the official-national Covid response of Donald Trump's and then Joe Biden's presidential administrations. It succeeded by using "we" as a method of coercion.

* * *

This chapter takes as axiomatic that "we" are not in this together nor do "we" have the tools. Claiming either is a pure instance of rhetorical manipulation. If observers have learned anything from the Covid response in the United States, it's the extent to which private solutions remain the neoliberal answer to not only public problems but even global crises like a viral pandemic.

But it wasn't always this way, and it didn't have to be this way, and I want to take us back now to the earliest months of the pandemic, when there was, in fact, a "we" – and it wasn't gaslighting to say so. In the beginning, as David Wallace-Wells recalls, "the solidarity was breathtaking."[5] All sorts of people across every identitarian axis took the pandemic seriously as an occasion to make a "breach with the status quo"[6] and to rethink "what it means to be human."[7] As writer-activist Vicky Osterweil recalls, we "overwhelmingly [wanted] to take care of one another ... launched into projects of mutual aid [and] thought carefully and lovingly about what we [could] do to support our neighbors."[8]

At the start of the Covid pandemic, it did in fact seem that the entire world was in it together, prepared to act in concert, and ready to shut down in unison for the greater good. It didn't matter if you were Italian or American or Kenyan – Tom Hanks or Joe the Plumber. Nobody had immunity, and "we" were aware of our shared human vulnerability to the coronavirus. To be sure: Hanks could quarantine at home, while Joe had to go to work. But for a brief, glimmering moment, it seemed that "essential workers" might actually be treated as essential, not expendable, and that the least privileged among us might finally get their due. There were no vaccines, and so there was no vaccine apartheid. Expensive, inaccessible prophylactics hadn't been developed, and so "the tools" hadn't yet been hoarded by the few, while remaining inaccessible to the many. (Since November 2023, the retail price for Paxlovid in the United States has been roughly $1,400 before insurance.)[9]

I remember that time keenly – that feeling of possibility, the hope for radical change – because I wrote it down. In March 2020, I entered into a weekly epistolary exchange at the invitation of philosopher Chi Rainer Bornfree. The occasion was the pandemic. The foundation was our decade-long friendship, which began in 2009 in the doctoral program in Rhetoric at the University of California, Berkeley. Over a period of four years, Chi and I exchanged letters about the pandemic, our responses to it, and our readings of the evolving public discourse on Covid. We then edited and crafted our correspondence into a work of creative nonfiction called *The End Doesn't Happen All at Once*.[10]

The End was inspired by a prescient, much-cited April 2020 essay by writer Arundhati Roy, called "The Pandemic is a Portal." In that essay, Roy puts a challenge to the world:

> Historically, pandemics have forced humans to break with the past and imagine their world anew. This one is no different. It is a portal, a gateway between one world and the next. We can choose to walk through it, dragging the carcasses of our prejudice and hatred, our avarice, our data banks and dead ideas, our dead rivers and smoky skies behind us. Or we can walk through lightly, with little luggage, ready to imagine another world. And ready to fight for it.[11]

Chi and I were galvanized by Roy's vision of a portal to a new world. Like Roy, we felt keenly that "nothing could be worse than a return to normality." Others voiced similar sentiments. "At the very least, we should commit to this," cultural theorist Grant Farred urged, "there will be no return to normal."[12] "I think the longer we are home the more hope there is the world will change in giant ways," writer Pam Houston predicted.[13]

With this challenge in mind, Chi and I wrote 100 letter-essays between March 2020 and May 2024, signing them "C" and "R." Our letters became a kind of portal themselves: a textual vehicle through which to imagine ourselves into new jobs, cities, literary forms, modes of relation, and conceptions of the "I" forged through collaboration.

We were not the only ones to respond to the pandemic by experimenting with epistolary forms of collaborative writing – the affordances of which I discuss in Chapter 3. Thanks to the ease of electronic communication, writers all over the world spent 2020 exchanging "letters in lockdown,"[14] staging "conversations,"[15] writing "parallel diaries,"[16] and publishing "together apart." They – *we* – wrote in search of "communion,"[17] to "think together about what it means [to] build livable lives"[18] and to "redefine their relationships from afar."[19] They – *we* – used everything from Google docs and text threads, to sophisticated online storytelling platforms such as An Archive of Our Own (AO3) and Wattpad, in order to document the unfolding present. Numerous essays, edited volumes, special issues, online archives, and books – as well as podcasts, films, art installations, and other visual media – emerged from that time of fevered interlocution.

In retrospect, it makes perfect sense that so many of us were writing letters to each other and that our letters would be "one of the gifts to come out of this pandemic."[20] Covid made nearby people feel far away and brought far-away people near. It opened up new, lived experiences of globality, the transnational, and diasporic attachment. After years of abstract theoretical discourse on such topics, the virus forced us to reckon with the visceral realities of our simultaneously bordered and borderless world, and the consequences of our migration histories. In Rustom Bharucha's words, the virus was "cosmopolitan with a vengeance"[21] and made itself at home everywhere. Covid thus forced nearly everyone on earth to reckon with our shared human condition; it made a mockery of the fantasies of independence and autonomy.

However short-lived, the rupture of Covid generated a widespread commitment to collaboration, interdependence, and interlocution. We wanted to talk to each other. Those of us who were not immediately fighting for our lives wanted to inquire into the meaning of those lives, together. This is what C calls, in a letter dated June 8, 2021, the gift of having been given "new unanswerable questions to live."[22] Questions such as: What makes life livable (and for whom)? What forms of writing are adequate to this time? Whose stories must be told? "What [is] the point of saying anything right now?"[23] What "reevaluation of our priorities" might come out of the pandemic?[24] "What world is this?"[25] How do we change this world? "Can we learn to *unlearn* our habitual practices and imagined modes of expertise, and in the process, acquire a new humility?"[26] "If not now, when?"[27]

For religious studies scholars Jack Miles and Mark C. Taylor, the desire for interlocution took the form of writing of over 500,000 words of letters to each other, between March 2020 and January 2021. Miles and Taylor – both in their seventies, with over two dozen books between them – wrote daily. The resulting book, *A Friendship in Twilight: Lockdown Conversations on Death and Life*, explores philosophy (Hegel, Kierkegaard, Heidegger, and Derrida), their shared interests (the university, cancel culture, artificial intelligence, climate change, politics, basketball, gardening, hunting), and occasionally their personal lives.[28] *Friendship* is largely a meditation on mortality, written from the safety of the authors' desks. But there are moments of tenderness, wisdom, and concern for generations to come. Taylor's last letter closes with a question about what he should tell his students about the world they stand to inherit. "[H]ow honest should I be, how far into the darkness dare I take them?"[29]

In spring 2020, to stop herself from doomscrolling, Black feminist scholar-activist Robyn Maynard sent a letter to Michi Saagiig Nishnaabeg scholar-artist Leanne Betasamosake Simpson, searching for comradeship at the end of the world. Maynard and Simpson kept up their "record [of] relationality" until the November 2020 US election.[30] Like *Friendship*, the resulting book, *Rehearsals for Living*, is not only about Covid. It also takes on climate crisis, apocalypse and survival, and the continuities between slavery and colonization. Maynard and Simpson realize right away that their communities will be hit harder than others. "Who, exactly, is imagined as a human?" they ask. They commit to meeting the cosmopolitan virus with their own ethical practice of "homelessness," which involves a renunciation of property logics and the constant giving away of one's house.[31]

On March 26, 2020, English professor Pam Houston sent a letter to fellow-desert writer Amy Irvine, whom she had never met, at the behest of *Orion* magazine, for the online series "Together Apart." When the series was over, Houston and Irvine kept writing to each other. They built a friendship over two months of letters, later published as *Air Mail: Letters of Politics, Pandemics, and Place*. Because Houston and Irvine did not previously know each other, their correspondence centers on telling stories from their lives. They describe writing to each other as "two barn owls calling to each other across a starry sky" and the letters themselves as a "life raft of clarity," "as necessary as air," "sustaining beyond all reason."[32] Together, they imagine the world that might come after Covid: a world in which people "stop lying" and learn to genuinely "love each other," having revised their priorities, goals, and senses of self.[33] "Maybe post-Covid we will be more conscious," they muse.[34] "After all, what single thing could be better designed than this virus to show us what *me*-ism gone mad in America has wrought?"[35]

Books composed primarily in the early pandemic months could pose such questions and articulate such hopes. Their authors believed in the promise of Roy's portal; they believed that, as Robin D. G. Kelley writes, "the end of the world promises nothing except the chance to make the world anew."[36] Many writers were of course painfully aware of the losses wrought and exacerbated by Covid: "the loss of health, the loss of life, the loss of reason, the loss of facts, the loss of truth, the loss of morality, the loss of beauty, the loss of civility, the loss of community."[37] Many of us knew that the struggle was not against one virus but rather against "five hundred years of organized destruction."[38] Still, collaborative writing in the early pandemic months produced what Kate Zambreno called "a collective feeling" of solidarity and interdependence.[39]

Judith Butler put it this way: "Because certain conditions of life and living are laid bare by the circulation of the virus, we now have a chance to grasp our relations to the earth and to each other in sustaining ways."[40]

"Ours is a time tailor-made for utopian thinking," Farred observed.[41]

Never before had the world sat "so close to the possibility, at least, of such large-scale transformation," Maynard wrote.[42]

In Houston's words, "everything is possible beyond our wildest dreams."[43]

"We truly 'are all in this together,'" reflected oral historian Michelle Fishburne.[44]

* * *

The pandemic marked a period of awakening for the privileged classes, generally, and the Global North, specifically: all of those (all of *us*) who had previously been protected from capitalist violence and structural abandonment. Books by those thus awakened, such as Miles and Taylor, or Houston and Irvine, are consequently about the journey from darkness into light, from ignorance into awareness. They revel in "a new sense of global interconnection" and anticipate a world that is about to change for the better.[45] In the early months of the pandemic, numerous commentators believed that the global vaccination campaign would succeed and the world would "accept mask wearing as an obligation of public life."[46] Progressive Americans excitedly anticipated universal healthcare, public transportation, and action on the climate crisis.[47]

Zadie Smith dubbed the pandemic "the global humbling" and a time of "radical possibilities."[48] "Millions of people," she predicted, "won't easily forget what they have seen."[49]

In retrospect, Smith was right, which ironically explains what came after the solidarity of those first few pandemic months: the great gaslighting, or, in more sophisticated terms, the "sociological production of the end of the pandemic."[50] Slowly, and then all at once, the "we" that emerged in the early pandemic was co-opted and redeployed as a method of coercion.

"Are we all in this together?"[51]

Close observers began to doubt.

* * *

We now know without a doubt that the Covid pandemic deepened existing inequalities in the United States and around the world. A disproportionate toll fell on communities of color, Indigenous populations, migrants, the sick and disabled, the incarcerated, children, and the elderly: all those whom global capitalism deems, in Beatrice Adler-Bolton and Artie Vierkant's term, "surplus."[52] The effects of Covid were unevenly felt at every level – social, immunological, racial, geographic – and existing gaps between the haves and have-nots only widened as the pandemic progressed.

To be clear, and as I have already indicated, many of those writers to whom I have attributed hope, optimism, and faith in the portal (including Bornfree and myself) were also aware that the portal might shut. They knew – we knew – that the possible was only ever possible, not assured. We recognized that official state declarations of our "togetherness" in the absence of material actions for the greater good were coercive. As Fang Fang wrote in *Wuhan Diary*, "When you hear people say, 'We will sacrifice everything at any cost,' don't misunderstand 'we' as meaning 'us' – you are actually the 'cost.'"[53]

"No matter how many times the state says, 'We are in this together,'" Simpson wrote, "we know we most certainly are not."[54]

Indigenous organizers and disability activists, writers such as Maynard and Simpson, Adler-Bolton and Vierkant, were of course right to situate Covid in a long history of state-sanctioned violence and organized abandonment. In retrospect, however, I think some of the most perceptive critics of structural inequity may have underestimated how the pandemic was also shattering the illusions of privilege. Thus, they could write dismissively of "white" and "middle-class" people "isolat[ing] themselves in their houses with Netflix, grocery delivery, working their secure jobs from home *with complete confidence that their governments have their best interests in mind*."[55]

In fact, many of those same people saw the cracks in the façade of collectivity – and were radicalized by them. I'm thinking of writers such as Farred, Fishburne, Houston, Irvine, Miles, Smith, Taylor, Zambreno, and, for that matter, Bornfree and myself. None of us thought the monied powers had our "best interests in mind." As Houston wrote in a letter to Irvine, "One thing the pandemic has made crystal clear is exactly how much we are on our own."[56]

In this light, I want to suggest that what at first sounded naïve – relatively privileged people declaring "we are all in this together" – may actually have meant something else: *We are all in this together* insofar as we now finally see that *we are all on our own*. In other words, the realization among the protected classes in the Global North that we had *never* truly been "in this together" created an opening – a moment in which we might, at last, have recognized ourselves as part of the collective.

"I've never seen, in my own life-time, such strong attunement, across different publics, many for the first time, to the need to collectively craft responses to support and protect one another, and those long abandoned by the state," Maynard wrote.[57]

That moment of attunement – that overdue recognition of what marginalized communities had long known – *was* the portal. Not a portal to Roy's new world, maybe, but a portal through which the privileged could finally *see* what had always been apparent to everyone else: We need each other. We have to fight together. We won't make it alone.

* * *

At the time of this writing, the pandemic story is no longer one of possibility or portals. Rather, it is of the stubborn endurance of global vaccine apartheid ("we have the tools!"), the rise of the variants, the breadth and depth of long Covid, the erasure of Covid data, the dismantling of the pandemic welfare state, and the acquiescence to mass death and disability ("we are all in this together!").

In August 2024, Olympian Noah Lyles was taken away from the 200-meter track-and-field final in a wheelchair, wheezing and Covid-positive. Lyles had run the race despite having Covid and he won a bronze medal, sparking a rash of op-eds about how the virus is "endemic" now, and of course his fellow athletes didn't mind being exposed to the virus, because they would have made the same choice.[58]

In November 2024, president-elect Trump announced what would have previously been an unthinkable series of Cabinet nominations, including vaccine skeptic Robert F. Kennedy, Jr., as head of the Department of Health and Human Services and Great Barrington Declaration-lead Jay Bhattacharya as head of the National Institutes of Health.

As I revise this sentence, it is January 2025, and across the United States, state legislatures are debating and enacting bans on masks.

Daily, the history of the pandemic is being forgotten, erased, and revised. In many communities, regular people have simply given up trying to protect themselves and others; they have unmasked and turned away. In Matthew Desmond's words, reflecting on the disappearance of the pandemic safety net established in the United States, "we have let it all slip away."[59]

But here, again, it begs asking: What part has "we" played in this – and what is we?

Reporting on a series of pandemic-era college suicides, Jordan Kisner observes that the pandemic state of affairs was always untenable: "more work than anyone could healthfully manage; less community resilience than people needed; anxiety about what variables the future might bring; and no sense of when it would end."[60] In the absence of honest public discourse, venues for mourning, and rituals of grief, individual people struggled to grapple with the scale of our collective loss. Meanwhile, the personal affronts mounted: being hauled back to work, losing a tax credit or unemployment insurance, your business shutting down, your child missing school, your student loan debt coming due, not being able to attend a grandparents' funeral, getting Covid at a wedding, a missed graduation, a dead neighbor, a disabled friend, your own long Covid, being gaslit by your boss, by the news media, by politicians and pundits, overwhelmed with technical information, overly expensive polymerase chain reaction (PCR) tests, inaccessible vaccines, getting kicked off Medicaid, vaccines that couldn't live up to their promise, the too muchness of your own life in the face of other people's, Twitter, capitalism, fascism, Trump . . . it was overwhelming. Some people gave up.

Here's how Vierkant puts it in the Death Panel's year-end account of "Covid Year Five":

> I think when we look back at . . . the last several years . . . to be quite frank some of our worst fears have come to pass. Rather than learning anything about our collective precarity and the need to take care of one another, the pandemic has instead been used to reinforce the narrower and narrower construction of risk and vulnerability, exacerbating a pre-pandemic fantasy of health where there are a set of so-called healthy people that are construed as the protagonists of society and then there are what is understood as a largely static minority pool of intrinsically unhealthy or intrinsically vulnerable people who society is simply not for, and additionally whose needs have been in the last few years presented as oppositional to the needs of the 'normal people.'[61]

So, who decided that the pandemic was over? Who ended the global health emergency? Who are these "normal people"? Who, pace Desmond, "let it all slip away"?

* * *

In 2020, there was a widely shared dream of collectivity. Forgetting the pandemic has meant forgetting that dream. As time has gone on, the hope of some "we" being in it together has given way to the reality of our failure to be a "we."

This is the context in which "we" is now being used as a method of coercion. Once more: I am not saying that there was no "we." The ironic tragedy of the Covid pandemic is that there was one. We glimpsed what "we" might look and feel like, and what it might mean to share the tools. And then we stepped through the wrong portal, away from the better future we could have had and the fuller "we" we might have been.

What if, in moving on from Covid, we left behind the world we wanted?

What do we need to remember – to make that impossible world possible again?

6

Of liberation

> No two abortion stories are the same, just as no two bodies are the same, but our storytellers share one thing in common: the liberation they experienced as a result of their abortion.
>
> We Testify[1]

> Would there was a plural for *her*.
>
> Abby Minor[2]

In 2022, the US Supreme Court's ruling in *Dobbs v. Jackson Women's Health Organization* undid the provisions of the 1973 ruling *Roe v. Wade*, which grounded the constitutional right to abortion in the United States in the right to privacy. In addition to enabling states such as Texas, where I currently live, to effectively ban all abortions, *Dobbs* exposed the fundamental limitations of *Roe*. Having relied on privacy rights to make its pro-choice case, the *Roe* decision obscured "the *social* conditions within which women actually make choices, conditions related to sex, race, and class."[3] To use the terms with which this book is concerned, *Roe* made abortion into an "I" issue, when in fact it's a matter of "we."

But it wasn't just *Roe* that individualized abortion and, in the process, laid the groundwork for *Dobbs*. This chapter pursues a major, more general contradiction at the heart of the contemporary fight to win and maintain abortion rights in the United States. That is: While abortion is an incredibly common, routine procedure and choice made by "one in four" women, the reproductive rights movement has tended to rely on exceptional women to tell their "one" abortion story in order to make this case. From the 2015 Twitter campaign #ShoutYourAbortion to the Abortion Conversations Project, individual testimony has been at the heart of abortion rights advocacy for years. Even projects that enlist the plural subject, such as the National Network of Abortion Fund's "We Testify" initiative and Planned Parenthood's documentary *Ours to Tell*, essentially aggregate individual stories. Assessing the changing landscape of abortion storytelling in 2019, Moira Donegan declared a pro-choice victory in the culture war.[4] She situated pro-choice merchandising and storytelling within the long tradition of the feminist "confessional, with women speaking about their abortions in an effort to humanize and contextualize the issue." Donegan thought that "we" had finally succeeded in making the case for abortion by narrating the why's and when's of our many particular abortions.

At the time of this writing in spring 2025, it is painfully clear that the political strategy of confessional storytelling has had the ironic effect of stigmatizing and privatizing what is actually a common, often unremarkable, and potentially public experience. If Donegan's optimistic account had been right, the sheer number of people telling abortion stories should have reinforced the general understanding of abortion's ubiquity, normality, and even banality.[5] It should have been impossible for the anti-abortion movement to triumph as it currently has in the United States. In practice, however, individual stories have only provided rhetorical fuel for the anti-abortion movement's bad faith utilization of the "exception" as a supposedly adequate provision through which to ensure the constitutional acceptability of virtually total abortion bans.[6]

Consider the following case. On March 6, 2023, the Center for Reproductive Rights filed a lawsuit against the state of Texas – *Zurawski v. State of Texas* – initially on behalf of seven plaintiffs, five of whom were women denied abortion care under Texas's three state laws banning abortion. These laws are the Heartbeat Act (SB.8), which prohibits abortion after six weeks of pregnancy and includes a bounty-hunting provision; the Human Life Protection Act (HB.1280), which is a trigger ban outlawing abortion outright; and a pre-*Roe* criminal ban on abortion, last amended in 1925, that is now codified in the state's revised civil statutes. Doctors and "abettors" found in violation of these laws risk fines of $100,000, up to 99 years in prison, and revocation of their state medical licenses.

Technically, each law includes a provision for a "medical emergency/life of the mother" exception in which abortion care may be legally provided.[7] However, all of the injured plaintiffs in *Zurawski* (a group of 20 women who had sought care, plus two obstetrician-gynecologists) were denied abortions or had necessary care delayed despite medical emergencies. These denials resulted in their sustaining a wide range of injuries, including: life-threatening sepsis; permanent damage to reproductive organs; mortal danger to a fetus in cases of twin pregnancies in which selective reduction abortions were warranted; having to travel outside Texas for abortion care; forced hospital stays against their will; inability to fulfill prescriptions for medication abortion; and being forced to carry to term and birth a fetus with a proven anomaly incompatible with life (e.g. anencephaly), only to then have to watch the baby die after birth.

Over the course of the year during which *Zurawski* was tried, many of the plaintiffs – almost all married, white women – shared their heartrending stories with the courts, reporters, and news media. They were telling a very specific kind of abortion story: the story of an abortion denied.[8] Their testimony was historic: "the first women in the country since 1973 to testify in court about the impacts of a state abortion ban on their pregnancies."[9] The Center for Reproductive Rights made each plaintiff's personal story available online, and many family members, including husbands and mothers, provided Amicus Briefs for the trial.[10]

No two stories were the same, as per the epigraph, and yet everyone was telling the same story. In a country in which 24.7 percent of women will have had an abortion by age 45, each plaintiff's story was clearly not hers alone.[11] Today, abortions are denied to all sorts of people: women with ectopic pregnancies and molar pregnancies; people carrying embryos or fetuses that medical experts have determined will not live after birth; victims of sexual assault, incest, and rape; people who risk losing multiple potential fetuses and require selective reductions; women who risk dying themselves if they remain pregnant any longer. "Would there was a plural for *her*," as poet Abby Minor writes.

Zurawski v. State of Texas did not try to extend abortion access. It didn't seek to restore *Roe*. It didn't even advocate for exceptions in cases of rape and incest. In fact, the case was not really about abortion rights or reproductive justice at all. *Zurawski* was about the equal rights of pregnant people to receive emergency medical care. The lawsuit simply asked the state of Texas to clarify the scope of the allowed "exceptions" that were supposed to protect individual lives in the context of a collective ban. Absent that clarity, doctors had not been able or willing to provide abortion care even in cases of life-threatening emergencies.

On May 31, 2024, the Texas Supreme Court unanimously ruled against the plaintiffs. The court shifted blame and pointed fingers, stating that doctors who determine that a patient's "life is threatened . . . and you may die . . . [or] suffer substantial physical impairment" while at the same time refusing to provide abortion care because of the state's anti-abortion laws are "simply wrong in that legal assessment." In its ruling, the court did not mention by name a single one of the plaintiffs who had suffered medical injuries and shared her story with the world, with the exception of Amanda Zurawski. The court confirmed that Texas law requires pregnant people to carry fetuses to term even if they have conditions diagnosed as fatal. And the court decided that only one of the plaintiffs, Dr. Damla Karsan, had standing to sue.

The ruling clarified nothing. But it powerfully preserved the fiction of the "exception": the fantastical, implausible idea that the right pregnant person in just the right emergency with the right kind of story would have found the right doctor to preserve her life, right on time.

* * *

Fast forward a few weeks from the *Zurawski* ruling into summer 2024, when Kamala Harris was nominated as the Democratic

Party's candidate for US president. Whereas Joe Biden had been reluctant to even say the word "abortion," Harris had been the administration's lead on reproductive rights. Her campaign immediately began enlisting "abortion storytellers" at rallies, specifically women like Zurawski who could "speak about the agony of needing to terminate a pregnancy for medical reasons and, because of Dobbs, struggling to find help."[12]

I attended one of Harris's final campaign rallies, in Houston in late October. By that point, the Harris team had plainly decided that abortion was their best closing argument. Apart from short appearances by celebrities such as Willie Nelson and Beyoncé, the event was essentially a pro-choice rally, with numerous Texas women sharing gruesome details about the life-threatening impact of abortion bans. For example, Ondrea Cummings told the 30,000 spectators in Shell Energy Stadium how she endured "a partial lung collapse, two liters of infected fluid removed from [her] abdomen and an incision that ran from under [her] breast to [her] pelvic area." Overhead, a giant screen played a Harris campaign ad, featuring images of Cummings' scarred body, laid out on a hospital bed.[13]

The Harris campaign hoped that storytellers like Zurawski and Cummings would make an "emotional connection with voters."[14] We now know that their stories were not enough to deliver a win for the Democrats. For abortion storytellers, this loss was intensely personal. "If people don't care about abortion now, they're probably not going to care about it in future elections," Erin McCallum reflected. McCallum lost half her blood and almost lost her uterus when doctors in George delayed delivery of her nonviable fetus. But even after hearing her tell her story, her parents decided that the abortion law in Georgia was a local issue and really "not about politics."[15] An "I" problem, not a "we" one. Longtime Republicans, they voted for Trump.

The irony is that the vast majority of Americans *do* care about abortion and support abortion rights. So, how did Harris lose? An exhaustive postmortem on the 2024 US election is beyond the scope of this chapter (and there are myriad other factors that went into Harris's defeat). But let's consider the possibility that, as feminist activist Jessica Valenti argues, the Trump–Vance campaign's deceptions around returning the matter of abortion to the states "won them the presidency."[16] This theory points us to a larger problem that lies in the structure, form, and concept of the individual abortion story, whether of an abortion sought or of an abortion denied.

All abortion stories unfold in a space between failure and fantasy: inevitable failure to transform the public discourse or halt the attacks on reproductive rights; tantalizing fantasy that if we can just tell the right story, identify the right teller, and narrate it just the right way, the individual abortion story might move readers and listeners, change minds, sway judges, and win votes. In practice, however, the abortion story fails because it says too much. (*Nobody wants to read the word* transvaginal!) The abortion story fails because it says too little. (*Make it more visceral, more bloody, more* real.) The abortion story fails at the level of plot. (*What kind of motivation is* that?) The abortion story fails at the level of character. (*Playing victim; not sympathetic; first person or third?*) The abortion story fails in the way of every subaltern speaker's story, because of its receiver's structurally conditioned "incapacity to hear [in it] what we do not already know to know."[17]

Abortion stories promise redemption in the present but earn their tellers no lasting catharsis nor vindication.[18] Indeed, they often violate their tellers instead. "Sometimes I get haunted / by the wound of explanation," Minor writes, adding: "I went into a sadness after I told my 'story' for the tape recorder."[19] One of the plaintiffs testifying in *Zurawski* was so traumatized that while telling her story she vomited on the stand.[20]

The reception of the abortion story is also inevitably compromised by the ideological assessment of the pregnant person's identity and motives. And the stories themselves are mired in definitional and procedural mess. What qualifies as an abortion, anyway? Is a miscarriage an abortion? Is treatment for an ectopic pregnancy an abortion? Confusing the issue has long been a strategy of the anti-abortion movement: If you are not sure (or refuse to agree) what something *is*, it's that much harder to make an effective case for it.

According to the *Oxford English Dictionary*, an abortion is "the expulsion or removal from the womb of a developing embryo or fetus in the period before it is capable of independent survival, occurring as a result either of natural causes *or* of a deliberate act."

But also: An abortion is the "arrested or imperfect development of a structure."

And figuratively: the "failure or abandonment of a scheme or process."

Former usage: "a monstrosity"; "a person or thing not fully or properly formed."

As well as: "an ill-conceived or badly executed action or undertaking."

Early or premature. Spontaneous or deliberate. Literal or figural. Chosen or undergone. Arrested or ill-fated. Failed or abandoned. Imperfect. Ill-conceived. This tangled mess of significations has for years been exploited by anti-abortion policymakers and lawmakers, who operate from the sly, bad faith premise that there is no consensus on what an "abortion" is or when it should be legally permissible, but – they declare with confidence – *we all agree it's a monstrous thing, you see, this bad, sad word that even President Biden cannot bring himself to say.*[21]

Here's what the anti-abortion activists want listeners and readers of abortion stories to think they know: that abortion is private, individual, exceptional; *her* problem, not ours. Individual abortion stories thus unwittingly end up distracting from the social and directing attention toward the individual woman vomiting on the stand. They abstract from the collective body and pierce the flesh of the single womb.

Abortion stories have failed because they do not recognize and grapple with the enabling tension at the heart of abortion: the fact that it is "irreducibly individual *and* collective, embodied *and* social."[22] On the one hand, an abortion is always a declaration and practice of autonomy: "a radical act of self-care," in Amelia Bonow's words.[23] On the other hand, an abortion is always a fundamentally relational, and, pace McCallum's parents, political act. This tension may be inadvertently exposed by abortion storytellers – especially, again, if they don't reckon with it. In *Ours to Tell*, one of the interviewed subjects confidently declares that, "[Having an abortion] was one of the first major decisions I made with no consideration of anyone else." The next sentence she utters then entirely undercuts her own claim: "I knew that I needed to be the best mother that I could be to the children I had."[24]

Can the "I" narrating an individual abortion story ever successfully lobby for the rights of the collective "we" – or only for the right to an exception? To put a finer point on it, when might the sustained failure of many-I's (the plural "I") indicate the need for a different articulation of "we"? What if we could learn to narrate abortion as a collective choice, not an individual one?

To be clear: By "collective choice," I do not mean that abortion decisions are or should be undertaken by deliberative bodies and groups (cue "the death panels" of rabid conservative fearmongering). What I mean is twofold. First, that electing to have an abortion is a choice with shared, as opposed to singular, ramifications. In literature scholar Margaret Ronda's words, abortion is "an act of care and sustenance, one that further illuminates a whole realm of caregiving relations often obscured from view."[25] And second, that electing to have an abortion is a powerful way in which the individual enters into the collective, and that "I" comes to recognize itself as "we."

* * *

Long before *Dobbs* and the overturning of *Roe*, long before the election of Trump, there was the steady creep of "targeted restrictions on abortion providers," known as TRAP laws. But instead of making a strong and affirmative case for universal, unconditional abortion access (no matter who, no matter why), many nominally "pro-choice" people equivocated with self-defeating promises of "safe, legal, and rare" abortions and patronizing language regarding "women and their doctors."

All of this language belies the experience of so many women, so many pregnant people, so many of *us*. Here's one of my stories: In 2015, I had an abortion in consultation with nobody other than a receptionist at a Planned Parenthood clinic in Chicago. Maybe she was a nurse; maybe not. I didn't ask her credentials. It was a five-minute procedure with local anesthetic. Afterward, I stopped to buy ice-cream, which my toddler and I ate with gusto. It was not a trauma; it was not even an accident. In fact, I had gotten pregnant on purpose, and then regretted it. I thought back to how I'd felt when I'd been pregnant with my daughter: blessed. This time, I felt like the butt of my own joke. I called my insurance company, local hospital, and Planned Parenthood. My insurance would cover a hospital visit, but I'd have to wait two weeks, which was two weeks longer than I wanted to wait. Planned Parenthood gave me an appointment for the next morning at 8:15. I took it, and paid the $400.[26]

As I have written elsewhere, this is not the kind of story that any abortion rights advocate would encourage you to tell.[27] Not the kind of story you'd hear at a Harris rally. In fact, if you were to try to come up with the least sympathetic abortion story you could imagine, it would probably go something like that.

But what if that was not *my* story, but rather what Abby Minor calls "h/ours" – the plural form of "hers"?[28] How might such a story land if it were translated from the idiom of individual whim into the language of social structure? What if that was my daughter's abortion story – the story of how she was cared for at age three? Or my son's abortion story – the story of the preservation of the possibility of his life? Or what if it was my students' story – after taking my class years later? Or my colleague's – after we bonded over the resonances between our choices and lives?

In *Reproductive Acts*, Heather Latimer reads North American fiction and film in order to show that "all reproductive choices are grossly political."[29] She is particularly interested in texts that describe abortion as social, communal, and perhaps even "a universally feminine experience."[30] In her telling, what I earlier described as abortion's conceptual capaciousness (or, incoherence) is ironically what ensures its universality. Every human experience is different, but every human experience is ***human***. Every life is different, but every life is a practice of living, and every life is consummated in death. Abortion is not exceptional. Rather, as Ronda writes, it is "a part of feminized bodily life," simply one more thing

– like a first kiss, like graying hair, like a broken leg – "that happens, or can happen, in the unfolding of embodied experience: a kind of 'rain,' a kind of 'falling' away."[31] Abortion is every weed pulled up in a garden, every hedge trimmed, every flower's other, every seed planted – only some of which will ever grow.

"Abortion" is not one. Not one procedure, not one experience, not one definition. How then should we understand the value – and danger – of "a single story"?[32] How do we get from "hers" to "h/ours" – to the "we" of "one in four" as a method of liberation?

*   *   *

This chapter has primarily been interested in the limits of the dominant mode of individualized abortion storytelling currently employed by pro-choice and reproductive rights advocates. In closing, I want to highlight two projects that sight "we" as a method of liberation: one from the realm of activist politics, as recounted by the feminist theorist Carly Thomsen, and one from the realm of literature.

Activism, first. In 2006, the South Dakota state legislature passed "The Women's Health and Human Life Protection Act," which banned abortion without exceptions. In her research on the discourse around the passage of this act, Thomsen encountered a mode of abortion storytelling that surprised her. Unlike the narratives typically voiced in the Anglo-American media, Native women leaders in South Dakota's Indian Country were able to tell abortion stories that were not confessional revelations of individual trauma. Thomsen observed that "narratives of Native women's individual experiences with a crisis pregnancy were absent; instead, Native women defended abortion rights through stories of their lives, families, and traditions, consistently addressing broader issues that impact Native communities and pointing to possibilities for the use of narratives to disrupt dominant discourses."[33] When Native women said "privacy" they were referring to "a space of collectivity through which conversations and support can manifest." When Native women said "freedom" they were referring to "the freedom to speak, to live, and to believe in ways that whites and Christians have long worked to make impossible for Native people."[34] Abortion was never understood as a choice, nor as a right, but rather, in Kim TallBear's words, as "a responsibility that grew out of the power in women's bodies."[35]

The operative word here is responsibility. Not hers, nor mine, but "h/ours."

I first encountered Minor's coinage "h/ours" in Ronda's writing on the poetics of abortion. For Ronda, abortion is not only relational, as I have been stressing, but also deconstructive. Following the work of Sophie Lewis (discussed in Chapter 2), Ronda reads abortion as a powerful, even foundational act of "family abolition," one that "[refuses and unmakes] . . . the Family narrative . . . inverting its premises" while "illuminat[ing] other social forms of interdependence and purposeful living."[36]

This is why she is drawn to Minor's poems, which braid together the narratives of the poet, members of her matriline, and historical figures including a nineteenth-century abortion provider known as Madame Restell. In this way, Ronda argues, the poems' "prismatic, multivocal" perspectives powerfully perform interdependence, purposeful living, and living together. In Minor's work, the single story is everyone's story, and nobody's story is hers alone. Every abortion story does the work of motherhood and mothering: which is, in sculptor Bharti Kher's words, "a continuous transmission of memory,"[37] and, in poet Juliana Spahr's words, "this way I begin each day by holding out my hand and then all day long pass on."[38]

Every abortion story is "connected to feminized knowledge and storytelling across generations."[39] The operative word here is knowledge.[40] "H/ours."

What if abortion storytelling were reconceived as the sharing of knowledges, not anecdotes, and of collective wisdom, not personal experience? What if abortion storytelling were fundamentally a practice of "critically analyz[ing] the intricate relations between abortion and the social . . . to build better coalitions"?[41]

What if the people testifying in *Zurawski v. State of Texas* and at Harris's campaign rallies had not spoken primarily of their abortions denied in the past, but of the abortions to be denied to all of our descendants in the future, of those who will one day be hauled up on pregnancy-related criminal charges or stopped on the interstate under the pretext of suspected abortion trafficking? What if they'd told each other's abortion stories instead of their own? What if they'd offered speculative testimony, grounded in embodied knowledge? What if they spoke of *h/our* abortions?

What might we be liberated from then?

7

Of division

> You both experience this cut, which she keeps insisting is a joke, a joke stuck in her throat, and like any other injury, you watch it rupture along its suddenly exposed suture.
>
> Claudia Rankine[1]

Two years into the first term of Barack Obama's presidency, I got engaged to a man who grew up in the American Midwest. A white man – or, a man who presents as white. One side of his family is from Mississippi; they trace their ancestors back to the Jamestown settlers. Southern aristocrats, with status if not urban levels of wealth, they are landowning farmers in the poorest state in the country. For years, they grew cotton. Then, faced with competition from foreign-grown product, they switched to rice, soybeans, and catfish.

I've been married to this man for over a decade. We have two children, who, according to American racial logics, are *hybrid*, *ethnic*. My husband has a brother with a Korean wife, and they too have a mixed-race child, who looks East Asian. "She asked me how I feel about having a Korean grandchild," my mother-in-law tells me one day, noting with something like pride that in fact she has multiple mixed-race grandchildren. Though she does not quite say it, I think she likes what the children represent: the promise of a liberal, multicultural America. I nod in recognition, although those words – liberal, multicultural, America – mean something different to me.

"Did you ask her how she feels about her child having a white grandmother?" I respond. My mother-in-law appears taken aback.

White people cringe when you name them as such, because they are so used to being unmarked subjects.

What I want to ask is this: "Did you ask her how *we* feel about our children's whiteness?"

* * *

This chapter is about the use of "we" as a method of division: a method of "cutting," to adapt Claudia Rankine's words, that hastens the "rupture" of relationships, friendships, and the body politic. When used as a method of division, "we" separates, estranges, and renders asunder. It does not just enact present and future separation between the parties or subjects in question; it also activates an historical memory of inalienable difference. In the process, it advances an argument about the impossibility of rapprochement. It becomes a driving force of racial formation.

In other words, this chapter is about race. But before I proceed, let me stress that when I say "race" I am not talking about a biological fact, essence, or cultural unity. By that same token, and as work such as Rankine's powerfully shows, race is not merely a fiction or fantasy. Race is "an active social relation rather than a transhistorical abstraction."[2] In the United States, it is "a fundamental organizing principle of social stratification" that has "permeated all forms of social relations."[3] Race is constructed. Equally, it suffuses the social order.

In their work on racial formation in the United States, Michael Omi and Howard Winant elaborate "the sociohistorical process by which racial identities are created, lived out, transformed, and destroyed."[4] They argue that racialization unfolds as "the extension of racial meaning to a previously racially unclassified relationship, social practice, or group."[5] Building on this work, literature scholar Colleen Lye cautions that the focus on the extension of racial meaning risks construing race as simply the result or effect of racism. Instead, Lye stresses, racial formation must be understood in terms of specific historical and material conditions and processes. The 1965 Immigration and Nationality Act, for one example: It opened the proverbial door to the United

States to white-collar professionals and foreign students like my parents, from countries like India. The replacement of black Mississippi farmworkers with white guest workers from South Africa in an otherwise overwhelmingly anti-immigrant Trump era, for another.[6]

Had I asked the question on the tip of my tongue, I would have been enacting a cut between my mother-in-law and myself, allying instead with my sister-in-law, both of us standing apart from (if not against) white people. In this chapter, I want to contextualize this moment with reference to three texts that grapple with racial division in historical, material, and structural terms, activating the histories of slavery and colonialism, respectively: Rankine's generically hybrid books *Citizen: An American Lyric* and *Just Us: An American Conversation*, and E. M. Forster's 1924 novel *A Passage to India*. I am interested in these texts because they depict how everyday communicative exchanges propel their subjects and characters into a racialized understanding of themselves and their others. In the process, they point to the social processes and pasts that subtend racial logics.

Sometimes, as in the mundane conversation with which this chapter begins, what is not said is as significant as what is. In either case, the stage of relation is set. Implicitly or explicitly, subtly or violently, "we" is used as a method of division.

* * *

I first visited Indianola, Mississippi, in 2010. It reminded me of small-town India, with its deep-rooted local families, acute class consciousness, racialized division of labor, and almost tribal relations. My mother-in-law grew up next door to her grandmother's house and across the street from other close relatives. Some of my great-aunts and uncles still live in the same central Kerala village where they grew up. In the United States, there are tracks and differently colored people on either side of them. In India, caste discrimination persists, and its legacies are still being negotiated.

It was not that difficult to make myself at home in Mississippi because I recognized it. So, when a silver-haired matriarch said with a smile that I was turning the family into "the United Nations," I smiled back. And when a nonagenarian Mississippi man commented on the color of my hair – "Your hair," he said, "is mighty black" – I didn't decry the exoticism. I was accustomed to Indian family members commenting on appearance: who has gained weight; who is too thin; who is fair and lovely; who is darkest of them all. I knew that the really insidious prejudices take more nuanced form than overt gestures of racial assignment.

"Your hair is mighty black."

Yes, I was a curiosity in Mississippi, a brown woman among white people who the black women served. But how could I judge their incredulity over my visible otherness, when I was, at the same time, clearly appraising theirs?

* * *

The trouble with writing about race in America is that you have to write about whiteness, but, again, "white people don't like to be called white."[7] Their power resides in the ideological production of whiteness as normality, neutrality, universality, the "background" against which everyone else is "thrown." (Cue Zora Neale Hurston: "I feel most colored when I am thrown against a sharp white background.")[8]

After nearly a decade of visits to Mississippi, after the birth of my two mixed-race children, and after the head-spinning events of the first years of the first Trump presidency, I was tired of not being able to call white people white. I wrote an essay called "Ricky and Jim and Me" that was an exercise in naming whiteness through the stories of two men with whom I hitched a ride one night from O'Hare airport in Chicago, Illinois to State College, Pennsylvania. The essay was published in 2019 in an obscure para-academic journal; it included the scene with the nonagenarian.[9]

"Ricky and Jim and Me" is about the labor of writing about whiteness, when whiteness is so thoroughly structured by denial of its own existence. It is about the difficulty of disarticulating what is "white" from what is "American." (That's whiteness: the slippage, the fact that you're never sure.) It's also about my specifically racialized childhood growing up in California, in contradistinction to my ethnic childhood in the Indian American community, discussed in Chapter 1.

As a child, I was actually quite comfortable in my identity as a hyphenated American who traveled often to India and lived between worlds (my critical consciousness about the vexed politics of hyphenation would come later). But I nevertheless began cataloguing racially inflected encounters at an early age. I was around ten years old when a little white Girl Scout at a community fair in the Bay Area asked me if I spoke English. That five-second exchange inspired the first essay I ever published, "Why I Never Became a Girl Scout," and set me on the decades-long journey of identitarian disavowal, repudiation, and accented reading that is recounted in my academic monograph, *Overdetermined*.

The lived experience of race in the United States is often a matter of pronouns. Pronouns such as "you," "I," "me," "they," and "we" are how race is made to matter. *Your* hair is mighty black. Do *you* speak English? In popular parlance, we call these microaggressions. Rankine's *Citizen* is full of them, sourced from friends, colleagues, journalism, and the author's personal experience. At once "confessional and experimental," *Citizen* is a multimedia, collagist work of lyric poetry, elliptical anecdotes, essays, documentary artifacts, and images that center moments that the racialized subject is meant to ignore. It has been called "the most culturally significant book of American poetry" of the 2010s.[10]

Here are two examples of microaggressive encounters recounted in *Citizen*:

> When a woman you work with calls you by the name of another woman you work with, it is too much of a cliché not to laugh out loud with the friend beside you who says, oh no she didn't... Yes, and in your mail the apology note appears referring to "our mistake." Apparently your own invisibility is the real problem causing her confusion. This is how the apparatus she propels you into begins to multiply its meaning.[11]

> And when the woman with the multiple degrees says, I didn't know black women could get cancer, instinctively you take two steps back though all urgency leaves the possibility of any kind of relationship as you realize nowhere is where you will get from here.[12]

The first example unfolds through two successive denials. First, the white woman cannot see "you," cannot see the individual personhood of the woman of color. Second, she cannot see her own mistake, extending what should be "her" error through the possessive plural "our." Although "we" is not explicitly voiced here, there is undeniably a "we" at work, one that divides the two women from each other, as the generalized mistake of white innocence cannibalizes their possible relation.

In the second example, "black women" signifies the inhuman other against whom the woman with multiple degrees shores up the "we" to whom she implicitly belongs. This "we" not only excludes the listener but also enacts a cut, a forever-rupture, into "the possibility of any kind of relationship."

In an essay on the lyric tradition into and against which Rankine writes, literature scholar Kamran Javadizadeh observes how Rankine defamiliarizes and thus amplifies everyday experiences of racism with which many readers are already familiar: "[T]he reader is put in contact not with truths so shocking that they have been hidden from view but instead with experiences so common that we have become inured to seeing what shocks they regularly deliver."[13]

If you are a racialized subject in the United States, you will, throughout your life, absorb casual comments couched in colloquial speech and bathed in alibis of unintentionality that remind you of your place, your difference, how you are being tolerated, the lines you transgress at your peril. You will "take in things you don't want all the time."[14] "Do you speak English?" "Where are you from?" "I don't see color."[15] "Exactly, what do you mean?"[16] "What just happened? Did I hear what I thought I heard? Should I let it go? Am I making too much of it?"[17] "What did you say?"[18]

I can recount a lifetime of such moments. In searching for a form in which to thread together Ricky and Jim's stories with my own, I was inspired by *Citizen* to try to universalize "my" experience through the use of the second-person "you." I tried to take up Judith Butler's insight that "you never receive me apart from the grammar that establishes my availability to you."[19] And so, in addition to the stories set in Mississippi, I wrote passages like these:

> [I]n first grade you are invited to Rachel's house, where you eat boiled carrots and uncooked cookie dough, and though this for you is an experience of the exotic, you recognize it all the same because you have seen it written. Chicken soup, meatloaf, cookie dough: in diaspora, these are your daffodils . . .
>
> At Hindu weddings of Indian Americans with predominantly Indian guests, pundits translate rituals and mantras into one-liners and punch-lines for the sari-clad white Americans. You get used to explaining the fire, the seven steps, the shoe stealing, the red dot. You are asked to rename everything. Every word you speak is a translation . . .
>
> "Lahiri," you correct the academic who mispronounces the famous writer's name. Lahiri. Lahiri. Lahiri. Lahiri. You think that if you say it enough, he will hear you and, knowing that you know better than he does, he will hasten to correct himself. That's what you think.

When it was published, "Ricky and Jim and Me" circulated in a small corner of academe and among my family and friends. Then one day, I got an email from Bruce Robbins, a well-known, senior (white male) academic in literary studies. His Indian brother-in-law had apparently written a "letter to the editor" in response to my piece. It started like this:

> I frequently recoil at articles about race in the US written by Indians who qualify because of color – hair, skin, and eyes – but little else. Many Indians speak good English, are highly educated (I know it's a stereotype, but true), wealthy

> and don't give a rat's ass about other "poor immigrants or minorities" here. We, and I include myself here, are delighted we have made ourselves a comfortable nest egg . . . We have our cake and we delight in eating it.

The letter went on in this vein for another four paragraphs, continuing to interpellate me into the author's "we." Indian American model minorities shouldn't be writing about race, the author said. "We" can't speak alongside the experiences of black Americans because "90% of Indians here have never experienced the wrenching violence of deep poverty or discrimination." The only kind of racism "we" experience, he wrote dismissively, is "where are you from? curiosity."

This disciplining letter was offered as a caution from one Indian to another. It dismissed as "curiosity" what is in fact widely understood as a critical component of the American racial imaginary. The reality is that "where are you from?" is one of the most violent, microaggressive questions a person can be asked, and numerous writers have said as much. Elif Shafak, who was born in France to parents of Turkish origin and has lived in the US, Spain, and the UK, writes that the question has "always mattered" to her and is "deeply personal, albeit equally complicated. For a long time it was the one question I dreaded being asked."[20] For Aminatta Forna, the question is "so irksome, for so many reasons!"[21] In artist-critic Lawrence Abu Hamdan's audio documentary, *The Freedom of Speech Itself*, a London-based migrant's attempt to answer that seemingly simple question presages Abu Hamdan's brilliant elaboration of accent as a "biography of migration."[22] The inevitable extension of the question – "where are you *from* from?" – motivated poet Monica Youn's award-winning collection, *From From*.[23] I could go on.

The letter to the editor almost entirely missed the specificity of the stories I'd told. It was symptomatic of, in Beth Loffreda and Rankine's words, "the enduring American thing of seeing race solely as a white and black affair, of considering anti-black racism to be the scene where the real race stuff goes down. Which is accompanied by the trope of the discount: the one that fails to extend to other people of color an authentic fullness of experience, a myopia that renders them in the terms of the 'not really.'"[24] At the same time, the letter offered a version of a critique I had heard many times before, about the politics of speaking from a position of relative privilege – in this case, the privilege of caste, class, color, and migration history.

I was of two minds about it.

On the one hand, I knew that part of the power of Rankine's work in *Citizen*, the form of which I'd adapted, was that she had situated everyday racist microaggressions in the long afterlife of slavery. For example, in the book's powerful section on Serena Williams, the iconic tennis player widely considered to be the greatest of all time, Rankine describes Williams as caught up in "our ancient dramas" – scoring points on court, when white viewers feel she should be "working the land."[25] No matter what she does, Williams's body is "trapped in a racial imaginary."[26] Throughout *Citizen*, Rankine situates quotidian American anti-blackness in material, historical contexts. To return to an earlier example, the white woman's claim that black women cannot "get cancer" is patently absurd, until the reader recalls the history of violence against black women's bodies, including J. Marion Sims's horrific gynecological experiments on enslaved women, and the persistent, pronounced racial disparities in maternal mortality in the United States.[27]

On the other hand, I rejected the implication that someone "like me" was too privileged to be the object of racial formation or subject to an alienating racial imaginary in the United States. And I deeply resented being implicated in the letter-writer's "we" – which he was using to divide people like me from other immigrants and American minorities. I had specifically not analogized the violence of anti-blackness to the politics of Asian Americans' "forever foreignness." Rather, I had set out to understand the "intimate estrangement" between subjects hailed into the civilizational contest between East and West[28] – which is also to say, the colonial encounter that is an inescapable part of my own racialized American prehistory.

* * *

I take the phrase "intimate estrangement" from Edward Said's *Orientalism*, the ur-text in my field of postcolonial studies, which I discuss at greater length in Chapter 8. It is particularly apt as a description of the colonial social world represented in E. M. Forster's classic novel *A Passage to India*. *A Passage to India* is about the impossibility of intimacy between people from the East and people from the West, because imperialism kills the individuality that is a precondition for intimacy in the first place. The novel is full of vexed intersubjective encounters, on a micro scale, that draw our attention to a history of "entanglements and dependencies,"[29] "overlapping territories," and "intertwined" pasts that refuse to stay past, on a macro scale.[30]

In the opening pages, a group of Muslim professionals in British India chat about the possibility of forging friendships with the English. "[It] is possible in England," one speculates, but "impossible here."[31] Over the course of the novel, the question of possible friendship between the "natives" of occupied India and the occupying British drives the primary action of the narrative. Experiments in "social intimacy" between Indians and Brits result disastrously in accusations of sexual impropriety and a divisive court case. Famously, the novel ends with an emphatic rejection of the possibility of interracial friendship: "No, not yet... No, not here."[32]

The initial friendships in question are between Dr. Aziz and two Englishwomen, Mrs. Moore and Adela Quested, who have not yet been entirely assimilated into British colonial culture and want to see "the real India."[33] Adela believes that Aziz will "unlock his country for her"; in fact, she regards him "as 'India.'"[34] Aziz mistakes this interest as an overture of friendship, but Mrs. Moore and Adela think of Aziz primarily as an "Oriental guide."[35] To adapt Said's words, an "Oriental" man like Aziz is "first an Oriental and only second a man."[36] Aziz is equally guilty of thinking "civilizationally" about the British. As he gets to know the teacher Cyril Fielding, Aziz makes observations such as, "You are a most extraordinary race... Is it your climate, or what?"[37]

Reading exchanges like these, Forster's reader grasps how the world of British India is structured by "unequal relationship[s] between unequal interlocutors"[38] at both the level of the everyday exchange and at the level of imperial infrastructure. Ultimately, Aziz can only be India; Fielding can only be Britain. Adela can only be the innocent and arrogant West; Aziz can only be the inscrutable, misunderstood East. Each character is read by all the others as the product of a collective history: as someone whose life, behavior, and beliefs reflect "primitive explanatory category[ies]" such as Oriental, thanks to the overdetermining discursive machinery of Orientalism.[39]

What would it take for these characters to view each other as individuals? Each would have to be able to make a break with the past, to emerge new out of history, to be allowed to inhabit what T. S. Eliot, in his 1919 essay "Tradition and the Individual Talent," calls one's "contemporaneity." In *Culture and Imperialism*, Said notes that Eliot's essay, intended as "aesthetic" reflection, in fact exposes wider implications of the co-constitutive nature of past and present. He expands on what he takes to be Eliot's central claim: namely, that if "the historical sense involves a perception, not only of the pastness of the past, but of its presence," then "how we formulate or represent the past shapes our understanding and views of the present."[40] Our conception of the pastness of the past is central to how (and if) we understand our selves and other people as individuals.

Forster's characters cannot see each other as individuals because, like Rankine's cast of unnamed characters, they are all haunted by history. Again and again, to adapt Rankine's words, they "realize that [they do] not share historical knowledge with the persons to whom [they] are speaking."[41] As Rankine does in miniature, Forster writes many deeply discomfiting, stilted, and exploitive exchanges between the unequal Indians and British, who do not share historical knowledge. The pivotal scene of the novel even turns on what we might today understand as a microaggression ("What did you say?").

Here is what happens. Aziz and Adela are walking in the Marabar Caves, where Aziz is playing tour guide. Each is lost in a private reverie, until Adela asks Aziz about his personal life: "Have you one wife or more than one?"[42] The question shocks Aziz; far from neutral, it lays bare the "evaluative interpretations" that Adela is forming about Aziz and India.[43] He ducks alone into a cave, leaving Adela to wander alone into a different cave. Eventually, she runs away in fright, under the erroneous impression that she has been assaulted.

Until this point in the novel, Aziz has mistaken "hospitality," and the acceptance of hospitality, for intimacy.[44] Now, it becomes clear that there has been no intimacy, only the qualified estrangement, confusion, and lack of understanding that enables Adela to suspect her host of making "insulting advances."[45] The tenuous attachment forged between Aziz and Adela breaks down. Adela accuses Aziz of assault, setting in motion a trial and confirming words from early in the novel that now read as prophetic: "it is futile for men to initiate their own unity, they do but widen the gulfs between them by the attempt."[46] During the trial, Fielding defends Aziz, and yet "at the moment when he was throwing in his lot with Indians, he realized the profundity of the gulf that divided him from them."[47]

Both "initiating unity" and "throwing one's lot in with" are attempts at fashioning a "we." Both fail. At the novel's end, Forster doubles down on this point. East and West cannot meet; "No, not yet." As Said observes, the end of the novel leaves the reader "with a sense of the pathetic distance still separating 'us' from an Orient destined to bear its foreignness as a mark of its permanent estrangement from the West."[48]

* * *

A Passage to India is about colonial culture, East and West, the British and the Indians over whom they lord. But it's also about people who ambivalently desire intimacy with each other, who just want to be friends – and this is where the connection to Rankine becomes clear. After all, Rankine's work is not just about the American interracial encounter but more broadly about the sedimented pasts that underlie all encounters between historically interpellated individuals.

In *Citizen*, Rankine explains this interpellation with reference to a friend's distinction "between the 'historical self' and the 'self self'":

> By this she means you mostly interact as friends with mutual interest and, for the most part, compatible personalities; however, sometimes your historical selves, her white self and your black self, or your white self and her black self, arrive with the full force of your American positioning. Then you are standing face-to-face in seconds that wipe the affable smiles right from your mouths. What did you say? Instantaneously your attachment seems fragile, tenuous, subject to any transgression of your historical self. And though your joined personal histories are supposed to save you from misunderstandings, they usually cause you to understand all too well what is meant.[49]

What Rankine calls "American positioning" is weighted with histories of genocide and slavery, of Jim Crow and abortive civil rights. This positioning disrupts friendships, and it extends beyond the US context. To recast Forster's novel in Rankine's terms, the Indian and British historical selves cannot commune; each attempted "we" reveals the fragility of their attachments to each other. Their self selves are eclipsed by the historical selves by which they are permanently shadowed.[50]

In her follow-up to *Citizen*, the 2020 *Just Us*, Rankine tells a story that follows directly from this distinction. She recounts going with a white woman friend to see the Pulitzer Prize-winning play *Fairview* by the black American playwright Jackie Sibblies Drury. Toward the close of the play, white audience members are asked to get up on stage. Rankine's friend refuses to play along and remains sitting silently in her seat. In the moment, Rankine says little, but later on, she realizes that she feels betrayed and resentful on Drury's account. She wonders, "Is my identification with the playwright because she's black, or because she's a woman, or because she's an artist?"[51] When Rankine finally asks her friend why she didn't follow the playwright's instructions, the woman's response is telling: "I didn't want to."

"What do you care?" Rankine asks herself, revisiting the exchange and "the architecture of [her] intimacy" with her friend.[52] "How do we keep all the differences on the table and still call that a friendship?"[53] "From this moment forward how easily will the pronoun 'we' slip from my lips?"[54]

* * *

How easily does "we" slip from my lips – and what happens when it does?

Did you ask her how we *feel about our children's whiteness?*

This chapter has explored "we" as a method of dividing and rupturing relations by both ignoring and activating histories of difference that suffuse our daily lives and establish the grounds on which we stage our relations. Every day, the present realities of interracial friendships and partnerships are negotiated in the context of radically asymmetrical pasts. To be black or white, to be Indian or American or British, to be of East or West, is to be of a history, to be spoken by history, to have not one but plural selves. "We are all," as Loffreda and Rankine write, "no matter how little we like it, the bearers of unwanted and often shunned memory, of a history whose infiltrations are at times so stealthy we can pretend otherwise, and at times so loud we can't hear much of anything else."[55] In scholar and critical fabulist Saidiya Hartman's words: "we inhabit historical time [through] temporal entanglement, where the past, the present and the future, are not discrete and cut off from one another ... [rather, we] live the simultaneity of that entanglement."[56]

Histories of racial formation shadow our present selves. They can't be ignored because "[a]ny attempt to erase these differences ultimately destabilizes us."[57] For my part, what I might once have called my mother-in-law's or my husband's "whiteness" is also my children's. It is also therefore mine.

Can I learn to live in and with this temporal entanglement? Can we?

8

Of incorporation

> There is a difference between knowledge of other peoples and other times that is the result of understanding, compassion, careful study and analysis for their own sakes, and on the other hand knowledge – if that is what it is – that is part of an overall campaign of self-affirmation, belligerency and outright war.
>
> Edward Said[1]

> Other people's lives. They are not subsidiaries, they are not symbols, they are not to be collected.
>
> Teju Cole[2]

Halfway through Teju Cole's *Every Day is for the Thief*, the unnamed protagonist, recently arrived from New York, goes to a market in Lagos, Nigeria. The market excites him; he describes it as "the essence of the city . . . alive with possibility and danger."[3] As he navigates the "hysteria of car horns and engines" and haggles with vendors, he recounts a scene that unfolded in the market six weeks earlier. A young boy was accused of stealing. A "furious" mob gathered. The boy was stripped and doused in petrol; a tire was flung around his body; he was lit on fire and burned to death. Afterwards, the air was thick with the smell of "rubber, meat, and exhaust."[4]

It is an atrocious story. Even more atrocious is what follows: nothing. The crowd disperses. The story barely makes the news. Nothing to see here, least of all by the market, which has already "seen everything," the market whose appetites must be satisfied, the market that "must eat."[5] The narrator, too, moves on swiftly into the next chapter's musings on the writing life in Nigeria, then a trip to the National Museum, then a visit to a tony cultural center, and then drinks with a friend. He marvels that "fascinating" stories like the lynching of the boy, stories full of "literary" merit, "fly at [him] from all directions" in Lagos. The narrator laments the relative lack of "material" in the United States – where fictionists are stuck "writing divorce scenes symbolized by the very slow washing of dishes" – and contemplates returning permanently to Lagos to pursue a creative life.[6]

Published first in Nigeria in 2007, then internationally in 2011, *Every Day is for the Thief* is about the literary lives of middle-class, urban, Westernized, cosmopolitan Anglophones like the narrator and the economic privation of subjects like the boy in the market. It is about the trade in stories and the traffic in livelihoods, on the one hand, and the global art market and international division of labor, on the other hand. Throughout the novel, the relation between these fields – in the broadest terms, literature and the economy – is articulated through the cannibal metaphor of the eating market, which serves as a figure for both neoliberal capitalism and the narrator's literary representation of contemporary Lagos. The market eats the boy in the same way that capital eats labor in the same way that artists eat their subjects in the same way that all of us hungry readers consume stories of "other people's lives."

* * *

This chapter is about cannibalism, metaphorically speaking. It's about how "we" appropriates "you" or "them" in the name of "mine" and "ours" in ways that are, in Edward Said's words quoted in the epigraph, part of an overall campaign of self-affirmation. It's about how the "we" that we already know excludes, isolates, and divides may also be used as a violent method of *incorporation*: a method in which some "you" is invited to join up with the human "we" – but only on "my" terms.

Before I proceed, I want to say a bit more about cannibalism, which is a deeply symbolic preoccupation and index of social anxieties and fears, as well as an historically specific material practice. It is a concept I use advisedly. Ontologically speaking, "cannibalism acknowledges and performs sameness"; one body is incorporated into another. Epistemologically, however, "cannibalism constructs difference."[7] It is a figure for thinking about the relationship between self and other. Grammatically speaking, "we" cannibalizes the other who might not wish to be part of the first-person plural. I am interested in how this "we" then indexes a kind of vulnerability to incorporation, because of our voracious appetites for union with the other. To riff off Judith Butler, quoted in Chapter 4, we all suffer from the condition of being not only "addressable" but also ingestible.

"Cannibal" was once a racist accusation leveled by colonialists against the uncivilized, non-Western other, whose supposedly ritual consumption of human bodies signified his lack of humanity. In this way, cannibalism has been a code word for primitivity, indexing the supposed savagery and immutable alterity of the other. Cannibalism "constitutes the cultural" and "makes difference."[8] It figures in an evolutionary discourse about the progress of man.[9] Like *sati* (widow burning) or female genital mutilation, cannibalism has long served as an alibi for Western colonial and neocolonial interventions. It is a practice out of which the barbarian other must be civilized and Christianized.

But if cannibalism "once warned us about others," Jennifer Brown writes, "it now warns us about ourselves."[10] In *Columbus and Other Cannibals*, Jack D. Forbes theorizes cannibalism as Wetiko psychosis, a disease that involves "the consuming of another's life for one's own private purpose or profit."[11] The idea of cannibalism as sickness, psychosis, contagious disease, and/or mental, social, and spiritual disorder renders it potentially universal. It is found in the West and in Western civilization, yes, but it is not ultimately confined to the West because it is catching.

More specifically, then, cannibalism is a figure for the depredations of capital. Most definitions of capitalism already assume its consumptive effects, whether the remaking of human subjectivity and potentiality, the instrumentalization of the body, or, in the case of neoliberalism, the ingestion of the state by the market.

Marx famously describes how capital eats labor, while compelling the laborer to engage in his own self-consumption by bringing his "own hide to market." Capital has "an insatiable appetite," Marx writes; it is "dead labor, that vampire-like, only lives by sucking living labor, and lives the more, the more labor it sucks." The paradigmatic example of capitalism's cannibalistic appetites is its consumption of human lives and bodies in the Atlantic slave trade. As Saidiya Hartman writes, the enslaved person was "the prey hunted and the flesh eaten by the vampire of merchant capital."[12] In all of this, the only consolation is that, in pursuing the satisfaction of its appetites, capitalism fatally undermines (by eating) itself.

Cannibalism need not be obviously vampiric, of course; it can also be seemingly altruistic. Although he does not use this language, the diaspora theorist Daniel Boyarin discerns something that I read as cannibalistic in the cosmopolitanism of philosophers such as Martha Nussbaum and Kwame Anthony Appiah, who, despite their professed commitments to freedom, autonomy, and dignity, espouse a philosophy that reads as "almost 'disembodied universalism.'"[13] In the name of normatively shared values, this cosmopolitanism privileges the values of those in power, Boyarin charges. It has a "strong tendency to impose its own colonialist, individualist, neoliberal ethics on all the peoples and people of the world."[14] Again, we need only think of the history of colonial civilizing missions that oppressed "native" peoples all over the world in the name of supposedly universal values such as democracy, freedom, and individual liberty: you are always free to be your own subject, according to this imperial logic, as long as you are subject to me.

In the field of postcolonial literature, the most significant text for understanding this logic of incorporation as it structures the relationship between self and other is Said's 1978 *Orientalism*. In that work, Said shows that there is no "Orient" with any "ontological stability."[15] Rather, the category of the Orient is an historically emergent discursive construct. Orientalism is a body of theory and practice; a school of interpretation; a system of representations; a cultural and political apparatus; and a technology of knowledge and power. Reading works of eighteenth- and nineteenth-century Orientalist philology, history, literature, and cultural production, broadly defined, Said shows how colonial-era European scholars and writers produced "the Orient politically, sociologically, militarily, ideologically, scientifically, and imaginatively during the post-Enlightenment period."[16] "Knowledge" of the Orient in fact "*creates* the Orient, the Oriental, and his world" as an object to be studied, disciplined, and compared with the West as its inferior, shadow self.

An ironic example of the Orientalist mindset in the South Asian context is T. B. Macaulay's infamous 1835 "Minute on Indian Education."[17] In the Minute, Macaulay, an Anglicist, declares that while he has "no knowledge of either Sanskrit or Arabic," he has nevertheless formed "a correct estimate of their value" and can say without a doubt that "a single shelf of a good European library [is] worth the whole native literature of India and Arabia." Macaulay then argues that "the natives" (here, the people of India) cannot be left "to the influence of their own hereditary prejudices"; they must instead be educated in English. In this way, the British will be able to form a comprador class of middlemen-interpreters who are "Indian in blood and color, but English in tastes, in opinions, in morals and intellect." In classic colonialist fashion, Macaulay considers himself to be an expert interpreter of India; at the same time, he assumes that India is "radically incapable of interpreting itself."[18]

Orientalism constructs "us" and "them" as irreconcilably different, a dynamic I elaborated in Chapter 7's discussion of race. But while Orientalist thinking is of course racializing and divisive, it also operates in a distinctly cannibalistic mode, which is my specific interest in this chapter.

Over the years, I have taught sections of *Orientalism* to numerous undergraduate students. Many at first read Said's critique of Orientalism as if it is simply a critique of stereotypes and essentialist representations. They think that the work of identifying Orientalism consists of pointing to the reductiveness of characters like Princess Jasmine in Disney's *Aladdin*, and they assume that bad representations like Jasmine might be countered by good, better representations of "real" Oriental women.

In fact, however, as Said instructs us, "false" Orientalist representations cannot be countered by "true" ones because Orientalism is not a veridic discourse. There is no "truth" of the Orient to be recovered. Moreover, Orientalism is not a matter of ignorance. Orientalism emerges from the desire for knowledge of the other and the pursuit of an encounter with the other's truth. It is a project driven by a lust for proximity and intimacy, a quest for "a particular closeness."[19] "It *is*, rather than expresses, a certain *will* or *intention* to understand, in some cases to control, manipulate, *even to incorporate*, what is a manifestly different (or alternative and novel) world."[20]

What, then, is the cure for ignorance of the other, if knowledge of the other is to be understood as a will to essentialize, metabolize, and incorporate? This is a question I encourage my students to wrestle with. After Said's critique of Orientalism, we can no longer simply suggest salutary "exposure" to other cultures or "learning" about them via novels, films, and study abroad programs. We have to think critically about the privileged position of being able to travel from *here* to *there*, literally and virtually. Who gets to study another language, culture, or people? When does tourism become a cannibalistic practice of "eating up" the experiences, identities, images, and lives of others?[21] Who gets to say, like Marlow in Joseph Conrad's *Heart of Darkness*, "When I grow up I will go there"? We in the West, and in particular in the imperial core, have to be vigilant about our own desires to learn other languages, to embrace "world" religions, to assume a "pedagogical relation" to other countries and peoples – even as we continue to engage with others and the world.

We also have to be careful about how and when we choose to write from the perspective of others and, in the case of fictionists, depict characters from very different life-worlds than our own. This is a subject that has in recent years inspired a number of polemics on aesthetic freedom, from Lionel Shriver's critique of "identity politics" to Zadie Smith's "defense of fiction."[22] The sides in this debate are easily caricatured; few critics of literary and cultural appropriation would ever say, once and for all, that a fiction writer must stay in her identitarian lane. But, as Paisley

Rekdal explains, for some people "the question of creativity will always take second place to the enduring history of colonialism": "[This does] not mean that they are against free speech, but that they are interested in larger questions around freedom, which is the right of particular communities to control their stories and to demand that the majority no longer has automatic access to any subject matter it likes."[23] What are the stakes of a white heterosexual male writer's writing from the first-person perspective of a gay black man?[24] Why was Jeanine Cummins's novel *American Dirt*'s racist depiction of a "faceless brown mass" of Mexicans celebrated by her publisher as authentic?[25] Nancy Leong identifies as "identity capitalists" those whose appropriation of minority identities enables them to achieve various forms of material gain.[26] For Deborah Root, late capitalist cultural production, especially the international art market, is always already fundamentally cannibalistic in the way it consumes the cultural difference of exotic others.[27]

This is the subject of Cole's 2023 novel *Tremor*, which offers a telling follow-up to *Every Day is for the Thief* through its critique of the imperial logics that persist in structuring our inhabitance of the contemporary world. *Tremor* follows a photographer named Tunde as he teaches at Harvard, travels to Lagos, gives lectures on art, and contemplates love, loss, friendship, life, and death. Whereas the protagonist in *Every Day* is fairly callous about his relationship to and representation of people like the boy in the market, Tunde is consumed with questions about what he owes his photographic subjects, how to fulfill the "duty of care" he feels for his students, and how to reconcile his love of Western art and music with the West's appropriation of African history and culture.[28] Throughout the novel, he rehearses anxieties about art and appropriation – who can tell whose story?[29] – and meditates on the boundaries between self and other.

In an early scene, Tunde angers a street vendor selling wares on the curb by taking his photo without his permission. Recognizing that this small, unthinking action points to larger social and historical dynamics, Tunde then asks himself:

> How is one to live without owning others? Who is this world for? White people taught us that the world could be dominated by means of religion and warfare, collected for the sake of pleasure and scholarship, possessed through travel, and owned by anyone willing to claim and defend that ownership. How is one to live in a way that does not cannibalize the lives of others, that does not reduce them to mascots, objects of fascination, mere terms in the logic of a dominant culture?[30]

These questions strike at the heart of the Western aesthetic discourse on cultural difference as well as the ways in which the international art market traffics in non-Western cultural production. In exhibit after exhibit, Western curators use the exonerating language of "acquisition" to explain how, for example, a copper-alloy relief Benin plaque made between 1530 and 1570 ends up being part of the "Robert Owen Lehman Collection." Western auctions, collections, and museums have swallowed up the history, heritage, and ancestral property of peoples from all over the world. "The museum," Tunde says, "has for a long time loved other people's objects with a death grip."[31] As he ironically observes, even the authenticity of a work of African art when it appears for exhibition in the West is secured by the fact of its decontextualization from its original, often sacred or religious, context.

We in the West have been trained to recognize the potential of the other's *universality* but not the fact of the other's *humanity*. We grasp the value of the Taj Mahal, in other words, but not the worth of the laborers who built it. As a result – and this is Cole's point in *Tremor* – the West respects other people's art more than it values other people's lives (if, of course, they respect their art at all – and here I'm thinking of both Macaulay's "Minute" and the ongoing destruction of history, culture, and heritage in the Middle East due to endless wars waged and backed by the United States).

By way of another example, take Ayad Akhtar's Pulitzer Prize-winning play *Disgraced*. The play begins with a married couple in a domestic scene: Emily Hughes-Kapoor, whose paintings draw on the Islamic tradition, and her Muslim lawyer husband, Amir

Kapoor, who tries to quietly pass as a Hindu in order to advance in his law firm. Emily's paintings have just been selected for a major exhibition, and she is poised for success thanks to her canny appropriations of Islamic art. "The Renaissance is when we turned away from something bigger than ourselves," she holds forth in conversation with an appreciative Jewish curator. "That never happened in the Islamic tradition."[32] Meanwhile, at work, Amir is subjected to a campaign of Islamophobic scrutiny, discrimination, and guilt by association with dire personal and professional consequences.

Islamic art produced by Emily, a white woman? Desirable, marketable, universal.

A Muslim man as partner of a New York law firm, post-9/11? Undesirable, impossible, never.

Disgraced shows how the idea of universal humanity – "we" – can serve as an alibi for metabolizing otherness as if it were proper to the self. Emily desires and attempts to produce *Islamic* art; at the same time, she has convinced herself (and her audience) that she is simply speaking in an aesthetic idiom that belongs to everyone. She is rewarded with recognition from the American art world, which essentially endorses the idea that she is better able to represent the Islamic tradition than any Muslim artist could. In her critique of anthropological discourse, Trinh T. Minh-ha describes what an ethical encounter with the other would look like: "I may stubbornly turn around a foreign thing or turn it around to play with it, but I respect its realms of opaqueness."[33] Emily, we might conclude, does not respect the opacity of Islamic art.

This is textbook cultural appropriation. It is also, and to return to the cannibal metaphor, a form of what bell hooks famously called "eating the other." In her much-cited essay by that name, hooks describes how white male students at Yale pursue sexual encounters with women of color; they seek not only to "sexually possess the Other" but also "to be changed in some way by the encounter."[34] Like the Orientalist, who pursues the Orient out of a desire for proximity and intimacy (as opposed to distaste or hatred), these young men "believe their desire for contact represents a progressive change in white attitudes towards non-whites."[35] Their desire for contact, hooks elaborates, leads ultimately to a kind of "commodification" of the other's difference: "[It] promotes paradigms of consumption wherein whatever difference the Other inhabits is eradicated, *via* exchange, by a consumer cannibalism that not only displaces the Other but denies the significance of that Other's history through a process of decontextualization."[36]

It should be clear by now why hooks enlists cannibalism to specify whiteness as that which ingests, subsumes, incorporates, or metabolizes the other, or, conversely, as that which disappears into the body of the other so as to remake it in its image. An example of the former is the white appropriation of black music, as depicted in the 2020 film adaptation of August Wilson's 1982 play *Ma Rainey's Black Bottom*, which ends with a white band playing songs by an uncredited black musician. An example of the latter is blackface minstrelsy, a practice powerfully critiqued via the white characters' assumption of black bodies in Jordan Peele's 2017 film *Get Out*. In both films, whiteness is conceptualized as an appetite that can only be satisfied by an act of embodiment or masquerade.[37] In the former, difference is incorporated and displayed; in the latter, difference is occupied and disappeared. The cannibal metaphor alerts us to the continuity between the performance/display of otherness, on the one hand, and its negation/elimination, on the other.

* * *

The title of hooks' famous essay – "eating the other" – anticipates the work of contemporary scholars such as Kyla Wazana Tompkins, who theorizes eating as a material and cultural practice of boundary-crossing and consolidation, as well as a technology of racial formation.[38] As a social practice, eating is radically universal and radically particular, profoundly human and profoundly inhuman. Eating destabilizes distinctions between subject and object, as the one eating and the one being eaten are metabolically fused. And it returns us, in closing, to the figure of the eating market and the young boy who the Lagos market – and, for that matter, Cole's narrator – literally and metaphorically consumes.

The boy is neither a participant in his representation, nor is he saved by his appearance in *Every Day is for the Thief.* Indeed, he is already "meat" and "skeleton" before the reader even learns of him. Literature does not humanize the boy, nor does it humanize those who murder him, nor does it bring him back to life. At best, we readers are distant spectators to his suffering and death. At worst, we might mistake his story for a lesson: about the depravity of Nigeria, about our own supposed virtue, about the order of the world and our secure place within it.

With *Tremor,* Cole returns to this lesson and helps his reader unlearn it. At the center of the novel is an extended chapter that consists of 24 stories of different Lagosians: among them, women, men, professionals, victims, aspiring émigrés, students, musicians, returnees, an artist, and a radio host. These stories are told in the first person and addressed to various interlocutors. The radio host's story is one of the last, and it serves as a commentary on the larger representational project in which Cole has been engaged for years, and which Tunde is contemplating. "[The radio program] works because I know I am having a simultaneously light and serious interaction with a person whose life I know very little about," the host reflects. "Hosting has made me respect my fellow Lagosians. Every single person you see out there on the streets, every face in every crowd, is someone who has had to solve difficult problems today."[39]

We all live at the crossroads of our own and "other people's lives." The question is not whether we touch one another, but how: with the respect of distance, or the hunger for intimacy; with the acknowledgment of difference, or the quest for its incorporation.

What am I to you and you to me and what, again, is we?

The question is one of method.

9

Of forgetting

> It is good for everyone to know how to forget.
>
> Ernest Renan[1]

> *E Pluribus unum* might have been the first national mistake.
>
> Claudia Rankine[2]

I wrote the short essay that seeded this book – the first version of "What is 'We'?" – in December 2019. At the time, India's lower house of parliament was debating a "Citizenship Amendment Bill" (CAB) that would extend Indian citizenship to Buddhist, Christian, Hindu, Jain, Parsi, and Sikh migrants from neighboring countries such as Pakistan and Nepal – but specifically not to Muslims. They are not "us," shouted the bill's sponsors from Prime Minister Narendra Modi's Hindu-nationalist Bharatiya Janata Party. But this is not who "we" are, not our secular India, critics of the bill protested. The CAB was plainly unconstitutional; it violated the established principles for determining membership (read: citizenship) in the political community of India.[3] Nevertheless, it passed.

Meanwhile, versions of India's citizenship debate were resounding worldwide, from Brexit to Trump's border wall to the Syrian refugee crisis to China's mass detention of ethnic minorities. Who represents us and our interests? Who speaks for you, for me? *We* are not like *them*; we believe in secularism, climate change, women's rights. *They* are not like *us*; we believe in private property, gun rights, separation of church and state. *We* are for life and choice. This is *our* history, not theirs. *We* are better than this.

Five years have passed since I wrote those words. Once again, the most consequential arena in which "we" is being deployed is in the construction – and destruction – of national identity. In June 2024, despite electoral gains for the opposition party and its allies, Modi returned to power as prime minister of India for the third time. In July 2024, after an unprecedented conflict within the Democratic Party in the United States, the expected Trump–Biden race gave way to a new presidential contest between Donald Trump and Kamala Harris. All of that unfolded against the jingoistic backdrop of the Paris Olympics, which served up daily reminders that nationalism is always a comparative and competitive project.[4]

Then, in the final months of 2024, Trump was reelected. The French government collapsed. The German government collapsed. The Assad regime in Syria fell. In South Korea, the president declared martial law, was swiftly impeached, and removed from office. For 18 months and counting, the world has watched the livestreamed genocide of the Palestinian people in Gaza at the hands of Israel, armed by the United States. In just the first 100 days of the second Trump presidency, Trump's executive branch has declared war on US higher education, immigrants, and much of the state apparatus itself.

What – the question resounds anew – is "we"? What, for that matter, is a nation?

In his canonical 1882 lecture, "Qu'est-ce qu'une nation?" philosopher Ernest Renan argues that nations are characterized by a kind of spiritual "fusion" that connects people beyond considerations such as race, ethnicity, language, religion, geography, military interest, or economic interest. A nation cannot be reduced to or explained in any of those terms. Rather, what constitutes a nation is its people's substantive experience of, relationship to, inhabitance of, and aspirations for the past, present, and future. Renan distinguishes "nations" from other collectivities such as tribes, assemblies, empires, and confederations. The nation, he writes, is "a large-scale solidarity, constituted by the feeling of the sacrifices that one has made in the past and of those that one is prepared to make in the future." What makes a nation a nation is that its people have suffered, enjoyed, and hoped together. They share a history, the desire to live together in the now, and the will to perpetuate their heritage in times to come. Renan quotes a Spartan song to gloss this idea: "We are what you were; we will be what you are."[5] Put simply: What makes a people a nation is that they *want* to be a nation. They want to be "we."

Key to Renan's argument is this: The nation's people don't just want together; as per the epigraph, they also *forget* together. "Yet the essence of a nation is that all individuals have many things in common," Renan writes, "and also that they have forgotten many things."[6] In order for Israel to carry out its campaign of extermination, the historical contexts of its own establishment as a state must be forgotten. The Palestinian right to self-determination must be denied. In order for Modi to wield power and represent India internationally, his role in the Gujarat riots and ongoing acts of authoritarian overreach must be ignored.[7] The secular founding of India must be forgotten. The Islamic history of the region must be erased from the textbooks. In order for Trump to be reelected, his two impeachments, his 34 felony convictions, the decisions he actually made in his first term as president, and the threat of Project 2025, had to be forgotten. His proven record of lies was expunged.

Daily, we are asked to look away from history, from reality, from context – to unknow what we know and to ratify, in Rankine's terms, quoted in the second epigraph, our ongoing "national mistake" of trying to render many into one, in and beyond the United States.

This chapter is about that project of unknowing: how the nation depends on "we" functioning as a method of forgetting.

* * *

Over the years, multiple generations of theorists have taken up Renan's idea of the nation as a spiritual principle, especially those seeking to disarticulate the nation from the state and distinguish nationalism from patriotism. Benedict Anderson's 1983 *Imagined Communities*, for example, begins with a declaration of the nation's normative force: "[N]ation-ness is the most universally legitimate value in the political life of our time."[8] Anderson argues that national belonging came into being in eighteenth-century Western Europe against two major cultural systems that preceded it – religious communities and dynastic realms – and that the rise of print-capitalism was crucial to the imagining of the national community. Anderson offers the newspaper as a figure with which to conceive of the "homogenous, empty time" of an emergent nation comprising anonymous readers, all sharing in the "mass ceremony" of reading the daily broadsheet in new vernacular print languages.[9]

There is of course more to be said about Anderson's well-known argument that is beyond the scope of this chapter.[10] For our purposes, I am interested specifically in how Anderson takes up the provocations of Renan's essay. He characterizes the potent emotional attachments generated by the nation as a secular structure of feeling analogous to religious fervor. He also points out a curious and telling slippage in Renan's argument. In order to explain national forgetting, Renan had to deploy ideas of (forgotten) events that he knew his French readers would (ironically) remember: "Having to 'have already forgotten' tragedies of which one needs unceasingly to be 'reminded' turns out to be a characteristic device in the later construction of national genealogies."[11]

What cannot be remembered must be narrated, in other words, and it is only in narrating what we are meant to have forgotten that we remember to forget. To put a finer point on it, what the nation "forgets" is actually what the nation narrates to itself most insistently as that which must be continually disavowed. In this light, even the slogan "never again," adopted worldwide after the Holocaust, is an injunction to remember that which must not be repeated that, through its very insistence on memorialization, ends up forgetting all the ways in which it has already happened – indeed, is happening – again and again.

* * *

I was raised and educated in the United States. I realize now, at 40, how much of this nation's history I didn't learn in school, and how much I was taught that I was then encouraged to ignore. I can see how I was habituated into a practice of forgetting that which I might otherwise have known.

Growing up, I was constantly exposed to discourses of American exceptionalism: the idea of the United States as the universally legitimate protector of democracy and human rights. This discourse was on offer in books and movies, and voiced by teachers, academics, policymakers, and public figures. "This is the greatest country in the world," etcetera ad nauseum. "Nowhere else on earth – " etcetera ad nauseum. "Only in America – " etcetera ad nauseum.

In *The Myth of American Idealism*, Noam Chomsky and Nathan Robinson gloss this dominant ideology thus:

> The U.S. government is honorable. It is capable of *mistakes*, but not crimes . . . In discussion of international relations, the fundamental principle is that we are good – "we" being the government (on the totalitarian principle that state and people are one). "We" are benevolent, seeking peace and justice, though there may be errors in practice. "We" are foiled by villains who can't rise to our exalted level.[12]

The ideology of American exceptionalism is an ideology of forgetting. It operates in disregard of facts, reality, and the historical record. In fact, to quote Chomsky and Robinson again, the United States throughout its history "has typically acted with almost complete disregard for moral principle and the rule of law, except insofar as complying with the principle and law serves the interests of American elites."[13]

This is why the official discourse obtains. I know that every time I heard stories of American exceptionalism as a child, they worked on me, encouraging me to unlearn what I had learned as a child of immigrants. Growing up, I traveled often to other countries, in particular India, and I knew very well that all people are people, and every nation is a nation, like any other. No exception(al)s.

This – "the extreme contingency of culture" – is what Zadie Smith, writing in 2008, hoped the many-voiced Barack Obama, with his roots in and routes through Kansas, Kenya, Hawai'i, and Indonesia, might enjoin the United States to remember, while being mindful not to "mistake the happy accident of his own cultural sensibilities for a set of natural laws, suitable for general application."[14]

I knew better. (Obama should have known better.) Still, the discourse of American exceptionalism seeps into our thinking. And even though I don't believe in or cathect to it, it inflects the position from which I think and write.

By way of a second example, in school, dates such as "1492" and "1776" were presented to us students as key periodizing markers signifying arrival, modernity, and the establishment of freedom. In order for such dates to take up residence in our minds, we had to forget many other things we had learned: the history of the peoples who already lived in continental North America before the arrival of the settler-colonists, for one; the fact that the Declaration of Independence only declared independence for certain kinds of people, for another.

Discussing Renan in his 2023 book on the diaspora nation, Daniel Boyarin observes that "slavery in the United States" is the paradigmatic example of a "discreditable [action] of the nation in the past" that must be forgotten.[15] In *Tremor*, discussed in Chapter 8, Teju Cole makes a similar point with respect to J. M. W. Turner's 1840 painting of the British slave ship *Zong*: "[We] must forget the *Slave Ship* in the way we must forget many difficult things with the kind of forgetfulness that allows us to keep on living our lives."[16] As legal scholar Patricia Williams notes, "To acknowledge slavery is to acknowledge our collective vulnerability and this leaves us all scrambling for an exoskeleton to call home."[17]

The United States is never quite what it says it is, because it cannot recognize its past. In the words of poet Alicia Ostriker: "we are not what we were / we will not be what we are."[18] But in the very moment that the nation's past is forgotten, its boundaries are also crossed: by those who refuse to abide by the limits of its "we" or accept its fantasies of exceptionalism; equally, by those the nation endeavors to keep out.

In April 2022, as part of his campaign for election to the US Senate, J. D. Vance posted a 30-second political ad that began with two incendiary questions: "Are you a racist? Do you hate Mexicans?" A former US Marine and a graduate of Yale Law School, Vance came to national prominence with his 2016 memoir *Hillbilly Elegy*, which promised to translate the dreams and disaffection of working-class white Americans in greater Appalachia for their urban, multicultural counterparts on the coasts.[19] The book felicitously hit the shelves just as the American political establishment was struggling to understand the rise of Trump. Initially embraced by white liberals, Vance took a hard-right turn during the first Trump presidency. He was elected as the junior senator from the state of Ohio in 2023 and, after a dizzying ascension, was inaugurated as Trump's second vice president in January 2025.

In the "Are you a racist?" ad, Vance is standing on a grassy lawn, the blurred background of a suburban subdivision behind him. He smirks. He rehearses familiar Republican talking-points about "Joe Biden's open borders" that are "killing Ohioans" by bringing in "illegal drugs" and "more Democrat voters." After the aggressive second-person address of the opening questions, he then moves into the first person, noting, "I nearly lost my mother to the poison coming across our borders." The statement is a non sequitur (Vance's mother was a nurse addicted to prescription painkillers), but the intended assignment of blame is clear. From "you" and "I," the ad then closes with Vance spitting out two new, emphatically pronounced pronouns: "whatever *they* call us, *we* will put America first."[20]

Intuitively, it seems clear that the language of "us" and "them" excludes and divides, as discussed in Chapters 2 and 7. *We* are on the inside. *They* are on the outside: on the other side of the border, or missing from the town hall. Saying so, ignoring their presence, building the wall: these are the methods by which the nation's borders are drawn. As Neema Avashia, author of *Another Appalachia: Coming up Queer and Indian in a Mountain Place*, writes, "Vance's rendering of Appalachia – a region that includes 13 states and 423 counties – *does not include people like me*."[21]

The rhetoric in Vance's ad clearly excludes people like Avashia;

it divides "real" Americans seeking to "Make America Great Again" from their supposedly inauthentic others. What I want to underscore here is that Vance's ad also powerfully uses "we" as a method of forgetting, in Renan's sense. Like other white nationalists, American nationalists, national conservatives, and members of the self-named "new right" (Vance calls himself an "America First Conservative"), Vance suffers from the delusion that James Baldwin once observed of America more generally: the delusion of thinking that the United States is "a white country."[22]

Countering such delusions was the impetus for the *New York Times*' 1619 Project, which proposed an alternate periodization and historical narrative for the "founding" of the United States, through numerous feature stories on slavery and its enduring afterlife.[23] "For hundreds of years, enslaved people were bought and sold in America," an interactive photo essay begins. "Today most of the sites of this trade are forgotten." For project founder Nikole Hannah-Jones, the goal of the 1619 Project was not only correcting and expanding the historical record but also communicating clearly to readers that the history of black Americans is worthy of memorialization, celebration, and remembrance. The aim was to "really reckon with our true identity as a country and who we really are" and "to understand the pivotal role that [black Americans] have played in this country."[24]

After its 2019 publication, many historians offered corrections to the 1619 Project and debated its presentation of certain facts.[25] This critical work was in the spirit of the project itself, which aimed at a more nuanced and accurate historical archive. At the same time, numerous conservative detractors and policymakers rejected, censored, and tried to outlaw the teaching of the 1619 Project in American schools – precisely because of its refusal to forget what has been deemed too threatening to remember.

The 1619 Project tells a story that has been suppressed; in this way, it disrupts what postcolonial theorist Homi Bhabha would term the "pedagogy" of official-national discourse. Writing after Renan and Anderson, Bhabha theorized the nation as emerging through narration: as a "form of cultural *elaboration*" that unfolds in time.[26] For Bhabha, the temporality of nation as narration is both pedagogic and performative. "The people are the historical 'objects' of a nationalist pedagogy," he writes; at the same time, they are also "the [performative] 'subjects' of a process of signification" that disrupts and subverts the pedagogy of the nation.[27]

Jones's performative "1619 Project" resists the pedagogy of Vance's "Are you a racist?" ad. Both are combatants in a rhetorical war of national narratives that are "often violently incompatible yet . . . laid over each other, co-existing within the same bodies."[28]

* * *

I want to turn now to the urgent context of the ongoing destruction of the Palestinian nation-people by the Israeli state. This is another instance in which "violently incompatible" narratives are at war, and a people's very existence hangs in the balance. As I type these words, the official death toll in Gaza resulting from over a year of annihilatory violence is over 62,000 (which is plainly an undercount). Tens of thousands more are starving, injured, and diseased; millions are enduring the destruction of their homes, lands, livelihoods, healthcare system, educational apparatus, entire bloodlines, and futures. All of this is happening under the alibi of needing to protect another nation-people, through, as scholar Marianne Hirsch writes, a weaponization of Holocaust memory that "authorizes retaliatory, eliminationist violence . . . under the guise of security and self-defense."[29]

Theorizing nation-thinking feels like a rather anemic response to the present conjuncture. But in this moment, this is the offering I am given to make. I am emboldened by the knowledge that many Americans – whose tax dollars are funding this genocide – and American Jews in particular have a highly charged but also ambivalent and ultimately mutable attachment to the state of Israel, which all people of conscience have a duty to interrogate.

In his 2023 "Jewish manifesto" titled *The No-State Solution*, Boyarin attempts to think his way out of what he describes as a deadly, "dead end" aporia. On the one hand, he is deeply committed to the growth, flourishing, and endurance of "the Jewish

People" as a people – specifically, as a *nation*. On the other hand, he is deeply committed to justice for Palestinians, which requires his full-throated rejection of the State of Israel. The solution Boyarin comes to, building on his own seminal, co-written 1993 essay "Diaspora," is that the Jewish People are a "Diaspora Nation": a nation that cannot and should not be consummated in the form of a nation-state, but is a nation nevertheless, as opposed to a race or religion.[30]

In order to make this argument, Boyarin first poses a question that will sound familiar to readers of this book: "What," he asks, "is the Jews?" Here's how he explains the significance of that seemingly ungrammatical question: "I am writing not of a collection of individuals who either call themselves or are called by others, or both, 'Jews,' but am asking about a collective identity . . . I am asking about a social entity and inquiring how that entity is best described . . . What is the Jews – a race, a nation, a religion, a gender, a sexuality?"[31] Boyarin pursues this question via readings of Talmud, historical scholarship, philosophy, Zionist tracts, postcolonial and diaspora theory, and public discourses. He argues that "the Jews" *is* a nation (again, not a religion or race) by dint of the fact that "the Jews" is "a collective that shares language forms, historical memories, ancient and modern literatures, practices of time and space, stories and customs."[32] A term such as "religion" cannot capture the nature, texture, form, or depth of this kind of collective belonging. This is a normative argument, and it hinges on the spiritualist definition of nation that is the legacy of thinkers such as Renan and Anderson.

For Boyarin, there are two critical concepts to understand here: diaspora and nation. To the former, Boyarin stresses that diasporic identity is not simply about dislocation, not necessarily tragic or pathological, and not essentially exilic in character. Rather, diaspora is a site "full of creative possibilities."[33] He writes: "Diaspora is not primarily an event in the past but an ongoing condition, a form of cultural national life in which nations may continue to exist, robustly, but the existence of and insistence on a piece of land that ideally incorporates only folks of that nation – and not only that, but all of them, or the vast majority of them

– is simply not in play."[34] I want to underline the phrase "ongoing condition." Like Renan, who focuses on the affective attachments of the nation's peoples to their shared visions of past and future, Boyarin's definition of the Diaspora Nation is ultimately about time, not space. It is about origins and destinations, yes, but not in terms of homelands, territories, or pieces of land. In the case of the Jews, Boyarin stresses, the condition of diaspora actually ensures his people's endurance, as it is safer not to have all of the nation-people living in a single territory.

Likewise, the nation of the Jews is a matter of genealogy and generation, not spatial location. Put simply, for Boyarin, the question of the Jews is a question of *family* – not the atomized neoliberal family discussed in Chapter 2, but family insofar as it is given, not chosen, and inherited, not elected. Thus, Boyarin characterizes the nation, and the Jews as nation, in familial terms: "[It] is the representations, the shared stories, the shared past – even if imagined – languages, modes of joking, practices on particular days and the like that add up to relations like those of lovers or siblings, that thicken the relations between people and produce a family-like sense of identification."[35] As a Diaspora Nation, the Jews in Boyarin's account need and deserve autonomy, but not sovereignty. They are a collectivity, but strictly not in racial, ethnic, or religious terms. Boyarin's goal is the preservation of forms of life and living that will enable the Jews to "retain its collective existence."[36] However, fundamentally, the Jews is not a collective that "is superior in essence" to any other collective, nation, or family.[37] Its rights do not trump any others. Thus, the "no-state" solution of the Diaspora Nation – a "we" that might serve both the Jews and the nation of Palestine.

* * *

I studied both diaspora and nationalism in graduate school, and on the way to earning my doctorate, I took a Qualifying Examination on "Philosophies and Problematizations of Nationalism and the Transnational." Toward the end of my study for those exams, I remember becoming rather exercised about a particular argument that Anderson makes in *The Spectre of Comparisons*, which was published a decade after *Imagined Communities*. The argument that troubled me was his critique of the figure of "the long-distance nationalist." Let me explain.

In *Spectre*, Anderson argues that all imaginings of collectivity involve some conception of seriality – of a series or group into which one can imagine oneself (or not). He draws a distinction between what he calls "unbound" and "bound" forms of seriality. Unbound series are collectives that anyone can join; they are definitionally "open to us if we wish to act on them."[38] The logic of the unbound is that the world is one; political activity is "common," happening everywhere irrespective of language, culture, religion, or economics. A "nationalist" is a nationalist everywhere; so too are "workers" and "prisoners." In a world of plural, "boundless, but grounded, universal series," I, too, can become " 'a' revolutionary."[39] Or, for that matter, an American.

By contrast, bound series have their roots in governmentality and are not open to others. For example, the census counts "Asian Americans" and "Pacific Islanders," the ranks of whom just any-"I" cannot join. Anderson denies the potentially universal content of bounded seriality because of this limit on who can join a bound series: "census-style, identitarian conception[s] of ethnicity . . . [lack] any universal grounding."[40] This claim then informs Anderson's critique of what he calls long-distance nationalism.

For Anderson, long-distance nationalism is a mode of "radically unaccountable" political identification, which flies in the face of the nineteenth-century nationalist project and is "a probably menacing portent for the future."[41] He describes it as a degraded project of First World migrants, cushioned in their home offices, sending guns via mouse-clicks to factions "back home," voting "here" but living (psychically) "there," marginalized "here" but "national heroes" there.[42] Long-distance nationalism, Anderson warns, is not the form of imagined political community and fellowship that characterizes Renan's universally legitimate nationalist project but something comparatively shallow and dangerous. The US-based Texas India Forum that organized the September 2019 "Howdy Modi!" rally in Houston, Texas comes to mind; so, too, do powerful lobbying organizations such as J-Street and the American Israel Public Affairs Committee.

Anderson's critique of long-distance nationalism proceeds from two assumptions: first, that nationalism is a universalistic project that operates through inclusive forms of "unbound seriality"; and second, that the modes of identification in diaspora resulting from histories of transnational migration lack universal grounding. His critique depends on the denial of the universal content of bound serialization as well as the conflation of "ethnic" and "diasporic" identities.

Revisiting Anderson now in light of Boyarin, it is evident what Anderson's theory of diaspora was missing and why it bothered me so much in graduate school. As Boyarin writes, "To be diasporic calls for taking care – not 'boosting,' 'supporting,' or being 'proud of' – both your nation and the folks of your locale who are not members of your nation and striving for the productive and just life for both collectives."[43] In this way, with this dual vocation, Boyarin attributes a universalistic dimension to forms of "bound" belonging without abandoning the aspiration of the nation form.

At the same time, I also recognize more clearly now that Anderson was right to be worried about uncritical long-distance allegiances to nation-states – not simply because the states in question are elsewhere, but more specifically because the hyphenated articulation of nation and state is too often left unchallenged.

What, again, is a nation – or rather, what might it be? A "we" that dreams of a shared history and reaches in tandem toward the future. A collectivity stitched from memory and labor, desire and hope. Equally, a "we" that honors the existence of other "we's" with other histories and ambitions that are as essential, fundamental, deeply felt, and vital as our own.

The project of imagining the nation does not have to serve the state. And sometimes, as Boyarin reminds us, it must imagine against it.

Never forget.

10

Of remembering

"We are children of Earth. Who are they?"
Reid Gómez, quoting John Trudell[1]

try to remember / what it was you loved
Jorie Graham[2]

On November 1, 2020, my grandmother died. I called her "Patti," a Tamil word for "grandmother." Patti, who taught me my letters and the names of the stars.

Patti was the third of my grandparents to leave this earth – or rather, in the spirit of Reid Gómez's citation, to return to it. But she was the first who had been my friend, and when she passed away, I felt a kind of grief with which I had never before been acquainted. It was a piece of the grief of extinction that poet Jorie Graham anticipates for all of us in her end-times poetry collection, *To 2040*. It was inflected with pandemic grief and internet grief and climate grief: the grief of not being able to travel to India for the funeral; the grief of having indulged in the convenience of distractedly texting Patti pictures over WhatsApp, instead of calling to talk to her; the grief of living in Arizona during the hottest year in the state's history; the grief of impossible distance, the grief of no return, and the grief of lost time.

I needed to mourn. I found myself obsessively rereading the email correspondence that Patti and I carried out between May 2007 and May 2015: all together, over 200 pages of daily news, recipes, stories about her dog, gossip about the neighbors, and complaints about the household help. It was intimate and mundane, urgent and extensive. And now it was over.

I wrote an essay about what Patti and I had shared. I called it "In Place of an Obituary." That essay is about who we were to each other. It guides what follows in this, the final chapter of this book, which is about having ancestors and being an ancestor, about having children and being a child, about the fate that awaits us all. It's about "we" as a method of remembering. I offer it in place of a conclusion.

* * *

The *Oxford English Dictionary* offers a long list of definitions of the verb "remember." Three stand out:

> "Remember": *to recollect; to think about; reflect on; to retain in or recall to memory;*
>
> "Remember": *to put together again; to reverse the dismembering of;*
>
> "Remember": *to commemorate; to retain some record of (an event, condition, etc.) in a way that affects future action.*

First, to remember is to recall. This is of course why I reread Patti's and my correspondence: to bring her voice and visage to mind; so as not to forget. I also wrote about Patti's emails as an act of re-membering: that is, in order to reconstruct her, to build up her vocal body, to put the pieces of our relationship back together, and to prevent it from falling apart. Finally, I read and wrote in service of producing a record that I could carry with me into the future, so that remembering Patti – and all my ancestors – would then mark how I move in the world.

To be clear: We don't normally refer to our grandparents as "ancestors." That term is typically reserved for those from whom we are separated by at least a few generations. Ancestors are like distant stars or underwater life: rumored yet real, absent yet present. All the same, for many writers, the ancestor is a vital muse. For the narrator of Maxine Hong Kingston's *The Woman Warrior*, the ancestor is one whose life potentially branches into her own, serving as a form of "ancestral help."[3] For Patricia Williams, to speak of one's ancestors is to speak of "the inheritance of linguistically and rhetorically embedded traditions passed on in habits of speech." "I am composed of the voices of those who bred me," she writes. "We are talked into the world by our forebears... Their accented soundscape is the familiarity through which we filter all experience."[4]

This is one vision of the ancestor: someone you claim and recognize as yours; the one to whom the popular T-shirt slogan refers, "I am my ancestor's wildest dreams." Equally, however, our ancestors could be those to whom we have an entirely abstract relation, not an intimate connection. They could even be folks we'd wish to disavow.

When my daughter was seven months old, we took her to Indianola, Mississippi, where her paternal grandmother's family has lived for generations. There, in a cemetery in Sunflower County, she bounced with a baby's reverence on her ancestors' graves. One was Alexander Calvin Pitts, her great-great-great-great-grandfather, born in 1841, the year Martin Van Buren was succeeded by William Henry Harrison as United States president. In India, where another line of her family tree extends, it was still the colonial era of T. B. Macaulay, whose prejudiced views on the "Orientals" are discussed in Chapter 8. Pitts could never have guessed that a little brown-skinned, Berkeley-born girl would one day call him kin. He might not have liked that. As my daughter learns the history of the American South, she might not, either. But the connection is there – both real and imaginary. It is a meaningful piece of fiction, like all connections.

In September 2022, a statue called "Ancestor" was commissioned by New York's Public Art Fund and installed in Central Park. It was Covid times; the sculptor, Bharti Kher, made it while she herself was suffering from long Covid. "Ancestor" is an 18-foot-tall sculpture of a woman with 24 heads attached to her body. It is legible as an Indian goddess, but it was also inspired by the Greek goddess Artemis of Ephesus. The statue appears weathered and has the texture of a clay pot that has been baking in the sun for a long time. It is beautiful and strong, on the one hand, and totally worn down, on the other. In interviews, Kher has said that the many heads of the goddess are at once "her children" and "her other selves."[5]

I want to underscore Kher's vision of the ancestor as one who has both descendants and other selves, who carries the weight of all those others and selves on her material person, and who is also always a descendant herself. My Patti was maybe too close to me to be my ancestor. But she is someone else's ancestor, certainly, and someone she might have known closely – a great-grandparent, say – is an ancestor to me. I am an ancestor. So are you. What might it mean to live, work, write, teach, and think in full knowledge of this form of our relation to both ourselves and others? As poet and historical geographer William Felepchuk writes, "Each student is a descendant and an ancestor; who am I to question / the loads they carry?"[6]

We would not exist without our ancestors; mostly, though, we exist without paying them mind. Or at least, some of us do.

It is by now commonplace to note that "we" in the West are cut off from our selves, our gods, our ancestors, and the earth. What else would explain the ecological devastation we have wrought? Cue the familiar, self-critical accounts of our "alienated" and "disenchanted" modernity according to Marx and Weber. In his writing on climate change, anthropologist-novelist Amitav Ghosh adds another term to this characterization of bourgeois Western moderns: "deranged." Ghosh observes that the spoils of industrial capitalism, "the patterns of life that modernity engenders," are not sustainable at scale and were never meant to extend throughout the world: "Every family in the world cannot have two cars, a washing machine, and a refrigerator – not because of technical or economic limitations but because humanity would asphyxiate in the process."[7] To think that we can keep going on like this, he writes, is pure derangement.

In *The Mushroom at the End of the World*, Anna Lowenhaupt Tsing also observes that "industrial progress has proved much more deadly to life on earth than anyone imagined a century ago"; as a result, "precarity" has become our universal condition.[8] The challenge now is to learn to live without the comfortable progressive narratives (read: lies) of capitalism. We must learn to tell different stories about who we are and where we came from and where we are going as a species. We must confront "the imaginative challenge of living without... [the] handrails of stories that tell where everyone is going and, also, why."[9]

For Ghosh, the project of telling new stories has two aspects: learning to think "the unthinkable," which is the task he sets out in *The Great Derangement*, and recognizing that nonhuman actors have always already been telling stories, too (it's just that some of us weren't listening). "What if the idea that Earth teems with other beings who act, communicate, tell stories, and make meaning is taken seriously?"[10] This question motivates *The Nutmeg's Curse*, in which Ghosh argues that nonhuman agents have always been with us, speaking through us, "think[ing] through us"[11] – maybe even "gardening" us.[12] The earth and the lands are alive, not inert; subjects not objects; variously "vibrant matter."[13] In Tsing's words, both non-humans and humans are engaged in "world-making projects"; "each organism changes everyone's world."[14] The key is to attend deeply to our relations, entanglements, collaborations, and contamination with others – to learn to think with "the presence and proximity of nonhuman interlocutors" and to plumb the depths of our "uncanny intimacy" with them.[15]

There are many such projects of unlearning and remembering ongoing. Tsing's elaboration of how we might "think with mushrooms," for one, but also Sumana Roy's exploration of "tree time" and Hannah Knox's work on "thinking like a climate" and Mel Chen's theorization of "animacies."[16] Building on philosophical scholarship about object-oriented ontologies and the posthuman, these works share an interest in the agencies, histories, and stories of the nonhuman. By that same token, in proposing that storytelling is not the sole province of the human, and in identifying the vitality of seemingly inert objects and the communicative force of the deceptively mute, these thinkers are rediscovering fire, so to speak. They are offering as *fresh* insights that are, from the perspective of other epistemological traditions, in fact rather obvious.[17] Ghosh's Anglophone addressee may need to be reminded that the earth is alive – his "we" may have forgotten – but it is equally true that another "we" already knows, never forgot, and remembers perfectly well who "we" are in relationship to the nonhuman.

My friend Reid Gómez, a scholar of slavery/colonization, has always impressed on me how central "land, gods, and ancestors" are to the traditions in which she works: feminist, Native American, Black Atlantic, human. "A long time ago," Gómez writes, "these white skinned people turned away from the earth. Everything to them was an object. They saw no life. They became afraid. They killed what they feared, and they feared everything. We are children of earth. Who are they?"[18]

Similarly, in *Rehearsals for Living*, discussed in Chapter 5, Robyn Maynard quotes filmmaker Ousmane Sembène's words on the devastation wrought by colonialists and imperialists, slaveholders and capitalists, Western and otherwise: "Everything they do is to destroy the land." Maynard then repeats those words as a refrain in her letters to Leanne Betasamosake Simpson – *everything they do is to destroy the land*. In contrast, she notes more than once, "We are the people of the lands."[19]

We are the people of the lands. We are children of earth. Who are they?

Such questions resound powerfully today, in the context of ongoing debates on whether or not "we" are living in "the Anthropocene."[20] In the simplest terms, the Anthropocene names the era in which the human has become a geological agent. For earth-systems scientists and stratigraphers, the term, coined by Paul Crutzen and Eugene Stoermer, denotes the geological time interval following the Holocene Epoch and specifies the material consequences of anthropogenic force on the earth. For humanistic critics, however, the Anthropocene names conjoined crises of politics, economics, ecology, and the social. Srinivas Aravamudan describes the Anthropocene as "[humanity's orchestration of] the peril of mass extinction through species suicide, ecological devastation, and planetary obliteration."[21] The Anthropocene is the era in which it is clear that there is no "nature" that is not already "culture"; in this era, the world is being treated as "a storehouse of resources for human interests."[22]

But whose world, and whose interests? If these definitions sound totalizing, that is because the Anthropocene is a universalizing discourse that assimilates all non-Western humans into "an abstract homogenous humanity."[23] On the one hand, the Anthropocene discourse marshals the undeniable rhetorical power of capital-M Man as a singular agent whose actions and inaction impact every being on earth. On the other hand, it unequally apportions responsibilities, rights, and sacrifices. As the postcolonial historian Dipesh Chakrabarty notes, we may share "one atmosphere," but "there is no politics that corresponds to planetary perspectives."[24] So: "Who is the 'we' of this process?"[25]

We are the people of the lands. We are children of earth.

Who are they, and what – again – is "we"?

* * *

All of us on earth are living with the consequences of "the tremendous acceleration brought about by the worldwide adoption of colonial methods of extraction."[26] Colonial-era rearrangements of land and lives – in addition to ongoing militarism, imperialist violence, and rapacious finance capitalism – continue to direct our movements, prospects, desires, and dreams. Put simply, it's the time of "end times fascism."[27] The world-endings that some communities have endured and survived for generations have now, finally, come for everyone else.[28] As the billionaire class makes plans to escape to Mars, we the earth-bound continue down the path of the sixth extinction and our inevitable "self-annihilation,"[29] phones and guns in hand. Our acute "solastalgia" – the distress caused by unfolding environmental change – is both a response to the climate crisis and a symptom of the fact that some of us have forgotten who we are.

Cue Natalie Diaz: "*Bone dry*, we say. Even though one-third of the weight / of a living bone is water. We know nothing / about ourselves."[30]

In this context, what would it take to remember what a bone is, what the world was, what, finally, "we" is – and what it might yet be?

Jorie Graham's *To 2040* responds to such questions. The 2023 poetry collection is about the immanent (in addition to imminent) end of the world, offered as an unflinching meditation on what it would have meant to be present to it. What if we had been present to the world. To ourselves. To all we are losing that, from the vantage of the future, we have already lost. What if we had lived.

Most of the poems in *To 2040* present questions as I have just done in the above paragraph: as facts or declarative statements, without question marks. If, to cite Gayatri Chakravorty Spivak's words that serve as one of the epigraphs to this book, "it is the task of the imagination to place a question mark upon the declarative," then Graham's project is to reconceive what imagination is, by removing question marks from statements we must now (whether we like it or not) receive as facts and certainties, as opposed to possibilities. Consider, for instance, the tone of this line in "I Am Still": "Old / story, have you ended."[31] Or, from "The Quiet": "Are we there yet you ask."[32] Without the openness of the interrogative, there is only one answer to what is no longer a question. The climate has changed. The world as it might have been is gone.

Graham's poems are "catachronic" in Aravamudan's sense of describing "a future proclaimed as determinate but that is of course not yet fully realized."[33] By way of an extended example, the opening poem of the collection, "Are We," includes many now-certainties: such as, "Are they / still here"; "What was / land / like. Did it move / through us"; "are you here"; "do you have a body"; "are your ancestors / real."[34] By projecting the speaker into the future in which we have already lost the present, Graham produces an exquisitely painful recognition of the fact that in the present we have already lost the future that we once wanted to have. We have already given up the world in which there could have existed "a real encounter / Of the old kind."[35] We are living in the time of the old kind now and it is disappearing as you read these words. We are in the world in which we no longer exist: "You / are barely here. The / raven left a / long time ago."[36]

Lest I make Graham's poetry sound cruel, it is in fact deeply compassionate, even forgiving. But it is the kind of forgiveness one extends when there is absolutely no possibility of redemption, which is to say, it is the forgiveness that is available only in the context of total failure. "Ah there is / no return / is there," the speaker observes in "Dusk in Drought."[37] Sometimes, Graham's speaker expresses this realization of loss in terms of her own first-person limitations, as in "Translation Rain": "It is a rain I have waited for all my life – / why do I see it only / now for what it / is . . ."[38] At other times, it is the collective first person "we" who must reckon with what we missed when "We used to speak of future."[39]

In the title poem, "To 2040," Graham departs from her otherwise elegiac mood to make an urgent call to action to the reader for whom – for the brief interval of a line of verse – it might not be too late: "You back there are you back there listening to me . . . don't forget to ask when your time comes for *presence* . . . . Place as much as you can in your heart . . . What was it, u must remember, what was yr message, what were u meant to pass on?"[40] This eleventh-hour call reemerges again in later poems: "try to remember / what it was you loved."[41] And, more mournfully, "let's try living here / one more time –."[42]

To 2040 speaks from and to the long-ago past and the faraway future; at the same time, these poems unfold (in) the absolute now. They ask us not only to imagine the world we once had, but to remember the world we have right now, this instant, from the inevitable vantage of our having given it up. As critic Christian Wessels writes, the poems enact the "immediacy" of "the near future, Anthropocene industry and loss" with "energetic bursts of syntax contending with their afterwards, their silence." In this light, the statement "I am alive" in the penultimate poem, "Dawn 2040," reads "not as a fact but a realization, a new kind of knowledge that could not have been understood before this moment."[43]

This kind of knowledge is "re-cognition" in Ghosh's terms: knowing again and anew. As Ghosh writes:

> The most important element of the word *recognition* thus lies in its first syllable, which harks back to something prior, an already existing awareness that makes possible the passage from ignorance to knowledge: a moment of recognition occurs when a prior awareness flashes before us, effecting an instant change in our understanding of that which is beheld. Yet this flash cannot appear spontaneously; it cannot disclose itself except in the presence of its lost other. The knowledge that results from recognition, then, is not of the same kind as the discovery of something new: it arises rather from a renewed reckoning with a potentiality that lies within oneself.[44]

It might seem counterintuitive to say that you can remember something you never knew or recognize someone you never met, but that is exactly what Ghosh is suggesting. To return to the story with which I opened this chapter, it's how I experienced rereading my grandmother Patti's emails. I'd forgotten many of the prayers she taught me, and some of the stories she'd told me, but I recognized through her words that I had known them once, because she did. I recognized her words, as Muriel Rukeyser writes, "as something already in [myself], but not discovered."[45]

One more example, if I may, with reference to a novel we have encountered in previous chapters. In *Tremor*, Teju Cole's narrator Tunde tells the story of the Micronesian navigator Pius Mau Piailug who sailed from Hawai'i to Tahiti by himself in 1976 without any instruments or guides, by tapping into a deep reservoir of "traditional knowledge." "Who is to say the universe is hostile?" Tunde reflects. "People like him show that a deeper intimacy with nature is possible and that this intimacy does not have to rely on the obliterative arrogance of Western culture."[46]

What is striking here is that Tunde doesn't want to have the explorer's knowledge as such. When Tunde "thinks about Mau he wants to change his own life."[47] He wants, like Mau, *to remember*.

One of the great lies of Western modernity is that "we" know more and better than our ancestors. We have the scientific knowledge, the technological advances, the tools, the internet, the stuff of futuristic dreams (and nightmares). When, in a self-critical mode, we do scrutinize the nature of this knowledge, we tend to fetishize the traditional, Indigenous epistemologies of native others elsewhere, way back in time. What is most urgent about the work of Ghosh, Tsing, Gómez, Cole, and Graham, among others, is their recognition that there are many people alive right now – our contemporaries, our comrades, maybe *you* – who are keeping the knowledge of the ancestors alive: knowledge of the earth and of what it means to be a child of earth; knowledge of other human and inhuman beings and of what it means to be a being among others.

They already know who they are – who we are. Which is to say, they know what and how and why to do with "we."

* * *

The preceding chapters have explored "we" as a method of inclusion and exclusion, communion and isolation, coercion and liberation, division and incorporation – with implications for how we understand community, family, race, reproductive freedom, and more. Each chapter has also, in its way, been concerned with questions of memory. Chapter 1, on inclusion, traced my efforts to uncover what community had meant before I unlearned it. Chapter 2, on exclusion, unmade what we think we know about family and belonging. Chapter 3, on communion, returned us to our deepest selves through epistolary exchanges with others. Chapter 4, on isolation, recalled what we once hoped for from the internet and social media, before they didn't deliver. Chapter 5, on coercion, exposed the machinery of forgetting that blocked our collective recognition of the pandemic as a portal to change. Chapter 6, on liberation, reclaimed the fundamentally social nature of abortion, too often miscast as an individual choice. Chapter 7, on division, reckoned with our inheritance of – and haunting by – histories of racial difference. Chapter 8, on incorporation, confronted the cannibalistic forgetting of the other's boundaries. And finally, Chapter 9 explored how the nation scripts the stories it must remember to forget.

In closing, I want to enlist a different vocabulary in thinking about our relationships to the past, to the future, and to our others – and about how we might yet use "we" as a method of remembering "I's" relations across time.

I am guided here by two strands of scholarship that differently deal with questions of intergenerational justice, inheritance, responsibilities, and rights. The first would have us recall that "we" are always already in relation to those who are not yet born – whose existence is fundamental to any meaningful effort to preserve the fate of humankind. In his incisive reading of Jürgen Habermas's model of a global constitutional order, for example, Michael Schwarz argues for a conception of a "we" that foregrounds its obligations to "future others of a global demos." He writes: "The actions of the current generation must not put future world citizens in a position that makes it more difficult or even impossible for them to fulfill their human rights obligations."[48]

Similarly, in "Taking the Future into Account," Michaela Bronstein describes our task as one of learning "how to see other times as requiring something of us today." She gives the example of the Future Library project, which started in Norway in 2014 and involves celebrated writers contributing new books to an archive that will not be read until 2114. Future Library is a call to action: a demand that we protect the world of the future reader, while sacrificing something in the present in the process. It is a challenge that "constructs a relation of generosity between present and future."[49]

Faced with accelerating ecological devastation and political crisis, it is clear that the future is at stake. But so, too, is the past, as literary theorist Sara Marcus poignantly points out. In her 2023 monograph, Marcus argues that we are living in the perpetual time of "political disappointment" – one in which our "longing for fundamental change . . . outlasts a historical moment when it might have been fulfilled."[50] Readers of this book know we have many reasons to be disappointed: the ongoing pandemic, for one; the loss of reproductive freedom, for another; racism, ethnonationalism, neoliberalism, climate crisis, attacks on democratic governance. There's plenty to mourn. But for Marcus, disappointment and "persistent unfulfilled desire" are "generative."[51] The key is to remember why one is disappointed, not to suppress it; to remember the change that one hoped for, not to forget it; to keep desire alive, not to deaden it. "To keep longing for a lost future is evidence of survival," she writes.[52] It is also a method by which we might constitute new collectivities and forge new solidarities, as we recall that we – in the present – are not the only ones who have been disappointed. What about those – in the past – who would have been disappointed in *their* future, which is to say, who might even feel they've been betrayed by us?

We have to remember the future we wanted, before we didn't get it, and who we wanted to be, before we weren't. This requires, Marcus writes, "caring for and listening to our ancestors," because:

> recognizing their untimely desires as linked with if not precisely cognate to our own locates us within a capacious, productive heritage of nonfulfillment and aspiration. Attending to the ways those we accept as forebears lingered with loss and found new forms and practices to accommodate, process, and transform their disappointment, we, too, can seek forms and practices suitable to our time, working in coalition with the dead as well as the living.[53]

In this way, the "shared experience of nonfulfillment" can become our "common ground," and whether or not we have the same goals, dreams, and desires, we can use the universality of disappointment to forge "a transformative collective."[54]

This work has to happen on every scale, from resisting the kind of gaslighting coercion we discussed in Chapter 5, to protesting the genocidal destruction of a nation-people, discussed in Chapter 9, to remembering how the internet's energies might yet be used differently, as discussed in Chapter 4. As Vicky Osterweil writes, the power-wielders would prefer us to be alienated and self-involved, divided and at odds: "They want us to forget that we overwhelmingly want to take care of one another." Instead, we must hold tightly to the recollection of moments of change that didn't happen, in the name of being "more creatively able to imagine that moment happening again." Remembering who we are is "an act of revolt" that involves "standing up for our own memories."[55]

* * *

Revisiting "In Place of an Obituary," I understand anew why, when my grandmother died, I wrote about our correspondence, rather than her life. I couldn't remember Patti outside of our relation – outside of how we addressed each other, who she was to me, and who we were together. Likewise, we cannot begin to combat the climate crisis or end-times fascism – or any other devastating aspect of our contemporary conjuncture – until we remember who we have been to the earth, and what it has always been for us.

"Everything is over now," Patti wrote to me in one of her final emails. "But we cannot forget."

"Do you remember," Graham writes.[56]

Well, do we?

Notes

INTRODUCTION: "WE" IS A METHOD

1. Kay Ryan, "Ideal Audience," in *The Niagara River* (New York: Grove Press, 2005), 28.
2. Amit Chaudhuri, "The Organic Intellectual, Mystical Poetry, and the Rationalist Tradition in India Today," *Social Research: An International Quarterly* 88:4 (2021), 985.
3. J. L. Austin, *How to Do Things with Words* (Cambridge, MA: Harvard University Press, 1975), 12.
4. Austin, *How to Do Things*, 30.
5. Zadie Smith, *Swing Time* (London: Hamish Hamilton, 2016), 116–17.
6. Robyn Maynard & Leanne Betasamosake Simpson, *Rehearsals for Living* (New York: Knopf, 2022), 239.
7. Kuan-Hsing Chen, *Asia as Method: Toward Deimperialization* (Durham, NC: Duke University Press, 2010), 215, emphasis added.
8. *Ibid.*, 212.
9. *Ibid.*
10. Judith Butler, *What World Is This? A Pandemic Phenomenology* (New York: Columbia University Press, 2022), 43.
11. Chi Rainer Bornfree & Ragini Tharoor Srinivasan, *The End Doesn't Happen All at Once: A Pandemic Memoir* (New Delhi: Aleph Book Company, 2025).
12. Ragini Tharoor Srinivasan, *Overdetermined: How Indian English Literature Becomes Ethnic, Postcolonial, and Anglophone* (New York: Columbia University Press, 2025).
13. Ashley Brock, "Can We Still Say 'We'? Manuel Puig and the Question of Readership in the Global Age," *Comparative Literature* 76:3 (2024), 356.
14. Vikram Chandra, "The Cult of Authenticity," *Boston Review* (2000).
15. Mark Chiang, *The Cultural Capital of Asian American Studies:*

Autonomy and Representation in the University (New York: NYU Press, 2009).

16. Hans Bernhard Schmid, *We, Together: The Social Ontology of Us* (Oxford: Oxford University Press, 2023). The book begins thus: "This book is about our being together. But who is 'we'?" (vii).
17. For Gayatri Chakravorty Spivak in *Death of a Discipline*, the question of "'Who are we?' – what kinds of collectivities are formed in the act of reading, in the classroom, in literary criticism" is central to the reinvigoration of comparative literature. See also Brock, "Can We Still Say 'We'?" 357.
18. See the language of the 2023 call for papers on "Critical Phenomenology of We," from *Puncta: Journal of Critical Phenomenology*: https://puncta.journals.villanova.edu/index.php/puncta/announcement/view/2.
19. Schmid, *We, Together*, vii.
20. Robyn Wiegman, *Object Lessons* (Durham, NC: Duke University Press, 2012), 13.
21. Donna Haraway, "Situated Knowledges: The Science Question in Feminism and the Privilege of Partial Perspective," *Feminist Studies* 14:3 (1988), 575–99.
22. Elif Shafak, *How to Stay Sane in an Age of Division* (London: Profile, 2020), 37.
23. *Ibid.*, 40.
24. *Ibid.*, 38.
25. Saikat Majumdar, "A Warm, Epistemic Caress," *Outlook* (July 18, 2019); https://www.outlookindia.com/magazine/story/business-news-a-warm-epistemic-caress/301944.
26. Nabeel Zuberi, "Listening while Muslim," *Popular Music* 36:1 (2017), 33–42; See also Pooja Rangan, Akshya Saxena, Ragini Tharoor Srinivasan, & Pavitra Sundar (eds.), *Thinking with an Accent: Toward a New Object, Method, and Practice* (Oakland: University of California Press, 2023).
27. Sophie Lewis, *Abolish the Family: A Manifesto for Care and Liberation* (London: Verso, 2022); Jane Ward, *The Tragedy of Heterosexuality* (New York: NYU Press, 2020).
28. Ernest Renan, "Qu'est-ce qu'une nation?" (What is a nation?), trans. Martin Thom, in Homi Bhabha (ed.), *Nation and Narration* (New York: Routledge, 1990 [1882]).
29. Joel Wainwright, "Praxis," *Rethinking Marxism* 34:1 (2022), 41–62.
30. Kiese Laymon, *How to Slowly Kill Yourself and Others in America*, revised edition (New York: Scribner, 2020), xv.
31. Mandana Chaffa, "Evie Shockley Searches for Humanity During these In-Between Times through Her Poems," *Electric Literature*

(April 25, 2023), https://electricliterature.com/evie-shockley-poems-book-suddenly-we/.

1 OF INCLUSION

1. David Palumbo-Liu, "Assumed Identities," *New Literary History* 31:4 (2000), 766.
2. *India Currents* is still in circulation and being published from the Bay Area at the time of this writing in 2025.
3. In 2022, the India Community Center's annual budget was reported to be $4 million. See https://www.indiacc.org/about-us/.
4. Ragini Tharoor Srinivasan, "Call It Community," *India Currents* (August 2007), https://indiacurrents.com/call-it-community/.
5. Rabindranath Tagore, "Visva Sahitya," *Rabindranath Tagore in the 21st Century*, ed. D. Banerji (New Delhi: Springer India, 2015 [1907]), 278.
6. Palumbo-Liu, "Assumed Identities," 765.
7. Walter Benn-Michaels, *The Trouble with Diversity: How We Learned to Love Identity and Ignore Inequality* (London: Picador: 2006).
8. Susan Koshy, "The Fiction of Asian American Literature," *Yale Journal of Criticism* 9 (1996), 315–46. See also Christopher Lee, *The Semblance of Identity: Aesthetic Mediation in Asian American Literature* (Stanford, CA: Stanford University Press, 2012).
9. Keeanga-Yamahtta Taylor, "The Defeat of Identity Politics," *New Yorker* (September 21, 2022), https://www.newyorker.com/books/under-review/the-defeat-of-identity-politics/.
10. Olúfémi Táíwò, *Elite Capture: How the Powerful Took Over Identity Politics* (Chicago: Haymarket, 2022).
11. Palumbo-Liu, "Assumed Identities," 766.
12. In addition to working as the editor of *India Currents* between 2007 and 2009, I wrote a monthly column for the magazine for 15 years (2001–2016).
13. The ethnic–mainstream distinction was still operative when I worked at *India Currents*, and so I use it to structure this discussion. At the time of this writing, however, the identity of "the mainstream media" is itself heavily contested. The newspapers and television shows of old are being replaced by podcasters, social media, YouTubers, and other new media platforms. See Helen Lewis, "The 'Mainstream Media' Has Already Lost," *The Atlantic* (December 5, 2024), https://www.theatlantic.com/magazine/archive/2025/01/joe-rogan-political-right-media-mainstream/680755/.
14. *Our Stories: An Introduction to South Asian America* (Philadelphia, PA: South Asian American Digital Archive, 2021).
15. Nancy Leong, *Identity Capitalists: The Powerful Insiders who Exploit*

Diversity to Maintain Inequality (Stanford, CA: Stanford University Press, 2021).

16. For an elaboration of accented reading, see Srinivasan, *Overdetermined*, in particular the introduction: "Identity and Other Open Secrets."
17. This story is also recounted in Ragini Tharoor Srinivasan, "Writing Ethnic in America," *India Currents* (2011), https://indiacurrents.com/writing-ethnic-in-america/.

2 OF EXCLUSION

1. Lewis, *Abolish the Family*, 4.
2. Louis Althusser, "Ideology and Ideological State Apparatuses (Notes toward an Investigation) [1969]," in *Lenin and Philosophy and Other Essays* (London: NLB: 1971), 149.
3. *Ibid.*, 153.
4. Judith Butler, *Gender Trouble* (London: Routledge: 1990).
5. Althusser, "Ideology," 169.
6. Michel Foucault, *Discipline and Punish: The Birth of the Prison* (*Surveiller et Punir: Naissance de la prison*), trans. Alan Sheridan (New York: Vintage, 1977), 103.
7. *Ibid.*, 202–3.
8. Michèle Barrett & Mary McIntosh, *The Anti-Social Family* (London: Verso, 1982), 43.
9. Lewis, *Abolish the Family*, 7. See also M. E. O'Brien, *Family Abolition: Capitalism and the Communizing of Care* (London: Pluto, 2023).
10. Friedrich Engels & Karl Marx, from "The Communist Manifesto," excerpted in *The Norton Anthology of Theory and Criticism*, 2nd edition (New York: Norton, 2010), 659.
11. Barrett & McIntosh, *Anti-Social Family*, 12.
12. Stephen Lee, "Family Separation as Slow Death," *Columbia Law Review* 119:8 (2019), 2319–84.
13. Kathi Weeks, "Abolition of the Family: The Most Infamous Feminist Proposal," *Feminist Theory* 24:3 (2023), 436.
14. Melinda Cooper, *Family Values: Between Neoliberalism and the New Social Conservatism* (New York: Zone Books, 2017).
15. Bruno Della Torre and Melinda Cooper, "The Holy Family: Neoliberalism and Neoconservatism in the Current Far-Right," *Cultural Dynamics* 34:3 (2022), 242–50.
16. Lewis, *Abolish the Family*, 57.
17. Arlie Hochschild with Anne Machung, *The Second Shift: Working Families and the Revolution at Home* (London: Penguin, 1989).

18. Pheng Cheah, "Biopower and the New International Division of Reproductive Labor," *boundary* 2 34:1 (2007), 79–113.
19. Cooper, *Family Values*, 7.
20. Barrett & McIntosh, *Anti-Social Family*, 46.
21. Lewis, *Abolish the Family*, 19.
22. Alexandra Kollontai, "Make Way for Winged Eros: A Letter to Working Youth," in A. Holt (ed.), *Selected Writings of Alexandra Kollontai* (New York: Norton, 1980).
23. Christina Sharpe, "Lose Your Kin," *The New Inquiry* (November 16, 2016), https://thenewinquiry.com/lose-your-kin/.
24. Merve Emre, "All Reproduction is Assisted," *Boston Review* (August 10, 2018), https://www.bostonreview.net/forum/merve-emre-reproduction/.
25. Kollontai, "Make Way," 291.
26. Raymond Williams, *Resources of Hope* (London: Verso, 1989).
27. Astra Taylor, *The Age of Insecurity: Coming Together as Things Fall Apart* (Toronto: House of Anansi Press, 2023).
28. Avram Alpert, *The Good-Enough Life* (Princeton, NJ: Princeton University Press, 2022).
29. Lewis, *Abolish the Family*, 5. This idea of exclusive accountability has in recent years been weaponized by the political right into bad faith demands for "parents' rights" when it comes to curricular decisions in public schools as well as vaccination requirements. These "rights" as construed by the right wing do not pertain to abortion care or gender-affirming medical care.
30. Pawan Dhingra, *Hyper Education: Why Good Schools, Good Grades, and Good Behavior Are Not Enough* (New York: NYU Press, 2020).
31. Barrett & McIntosh, *Anti-Social Family*, 56. Weeks also uses the language of "trap" in describing the "paradoxical existence" of the US family "as a narrow prescription and variable instantiation, a social expectation and a personal choice, a vicious trap and welcome sanctuary" (437).
32. Barrett & McIntosh, *Anti-Social Family*, 47.
33. Lewis, *Abolish the Family*, 83.
34. Arlie Hochschild, *So How's the Family? And Other Essays* (Oakland: University of California Press, 2013), 3.
35. Lewis, *Abolish the Family*, 4.
36. Barrett & McIntosh, *Anti-Social Family*, 21.
37. Cooper, *Family Values*, 9.
38. David Brooks, "The Nuclear Family Was a Mistake," *The Atlantic* (March 2020), https://www.theatlantic.com/magazine/archive/2020/03/the-nuclear-family-was-a-mistake/605536/.

39. Lewis, *Abolish the Family*, 81, 18.

3 OF COMMUNION

1. R. Radhakrishnan and Ragini Tharoor Srinivasan, "Thinking *Thinking Literature across Continents* across Generations," *Comparative Literature Studies* 55:4 (2018), 931–2.
2. For more on related transnational traditions of oral/aural, improvisatory "call and response," including the Native American talking circle, see Simone Muench and Dean Rader with Sally Ashton and Jackie White, *They Said: A Multi-genre Anthology of Contemporary Collaborative Writing* (New York: Black Lawrence Press, 2018).
3. Radhakrishnan & Srinivasan, "Thinking," 931–2.
4. Linda S. Kauffman, *Discourses of Desire: Gender, Genre, and Epistolary Fictions* (Ithaca, NY: Cornell University Press, 1988), 18.
5. Radhakrishnan & Srinivasan, "Thinking," 935.
6. *Ibid.*, 931.
7. Ross Gay, quoted in Anissa Wardi, "Elegiac Joy: Ross Gay and Aimee Nezhukumatathil's Poetics of the Garden," in Julia Fiedorczuk *et al.* (eds), *Routledge Companion to Ecopoetics* (Abingdon: Routledge, 2023), 136.
8. Rebecca Walkowitz, "On Not Knowing: Lahiri, Tawada, Ishiguro," *New Literary History* 51 (2020), 330.
9. For a lengthy analysis of Lahiri's turn to Italian, see Chapter 7 on Jhumpa Lahiri in Srinivasan, *Overdetermined*.
10. To be clear, there is a way in which all writing is collaborative, even single-authored texts penned in a writer's first (which is to say, mastered) language. There is always some future reader with whom the writer is already in dialogue. There is always some text to which the writer is delivering a belated response. All writing is collaborative, because all writing is referential, citational, and intertextual. In the words of the co-editors of *They Said*, "we are all already collaborating" all the time. See Muench & Rader, *They Said*, 2.
11. Jhumpa Lahiri, *In Other Words*, trans. Ann Goldstein (New York: Knopf, 2016), 35, 37, 221, 63.
12. *Ibid.*, 43.
13. *Ibid.*, 83, 213.
14. *Ibid.*, 21.
15. *Ibid.*, 95.
16. *Ibid.*, 173.
17. In recent years, co-written criticism has become a more popular and acceptable form of academic writing. See Sarah Chihaya, Merve Emre, Katherine Hill, & Juno Jill Richards, *The Ferrante Letters: An*

Experiment in Collective Criticism (New York: Columbia University Press, 2020); Sofia Samatar & Kate Zambreno, *Tone* (New York: Columbia University Press, 2023); and Maggie Laurel Boyd & Bekah Waalkes, "Reading Well with Others: The Book Club as Critical Method," *ASAP/Review* (April 15, 2024), https://asapjournal.com/feature/reading-well-with-others-the-book-club-as-critical-method/.

18. Muench & Rader, *They Said*, 1.
19. Natalie Diaz, "Isn't the Air Also a Body, Moving?" from "Envelopes of Air," *The New Yorker* (May 23, 2018), https://www.newyorker.com/books/poems/envelopes-of-air-ada-limon-and-natalie-diaz-forge-a-bond-amid-the-shifting-landscape-of-contemporary-america.
20. Ada Limón, "Sometimes I Think My Body Leaves a Shape in the Air," from "Envelopes of Air," *The New Yorker* (May 23, 2018), https://www.newyorker.com/books/poems/envelopes-of-air-ada-limon-and-natalie-diaz-forge-a-bond-amid-the-shifting-landscape-of-contemporary-america.
21. Frantz Fanon, *Black Skin, White Masks* (New York: Grove Press, 2008 [1952]), 1.
22. Ross Gay & Aimee Nezhukumatathil, *Lace and Pyrite: Letters from Two Gardens* (Detroit, MI: Organic Weapon Arts, 2014).
23. Wardi, "Elegiac Joy," 137.
24. Rushi Vyas & Rajiv Mohabir, *Between Us, Not Half a Saint* (Gilbert, AZ: Gasher Press, 2021).
25. See also Carla Harryman & Lyn Hejinian, *The Wide Road* (Brooklyn, NY: Belladonna Books, 2011). Harryman and Hejinian write toward a "we" in which their authorship is melded. The book includes both co-written work, essays by the individual authors, a series of letters exchanged over many years, and a two-column (or two-tone) section in which each writes right up against the other on the page.
26. Vyas & Mohabir, "Gayatri," 1.
27. Vyas & Mohabir, "Soca," 4.
28. "Ada Limón and Natalie Diaz Discuss 'Envelopes of Air' with Kevin Young," *New Yorker* (May 23, 2018), https://www.newyorker.com/podcast/poetry/ada-limon-and-natalie-diaz-discuss-envelopes-of-air/.
29. Limón, "Cargo," from "Envelopes of Air."
30. Limón, "From the Ash Inside the Bone," from "Envelopes of Air."
31. Limón, "Cargo," from "Envelopes of Air."
32. Diaz, "Isn't the Air also a Body, Moving?" and Limón, "Sway," from "Envelopes of Air."
33. Diaz, "That Which Cannot Be Stilled," from "Envelopes of Air."
34. Google "lost art of letter writing" and you'll get a zillion hits. Miranda

Sawyer, "The Lost Art of Letter Writing – and Why It Still Matters," *The Guardian* (December 10, 2023), https://www.theguardian.com/books/2023/dec/10/why-letters-still-matter-despite-all-our-instant-communication.

35. Divya Victor, "Cicadas in the Mouth," *Semblance: Two Essays* (Butte, MT: Sputnik & Fizzle, 2016), 29.

4 OF ISOLATION

1. Byung-Chul Han, *In the Swarm: Digital Prospects*, trans. Erik Butler (Cambridge, MA: MIT Press, 2017), 40.
2. See https://www.meta.com/metaverse/.
3. Blake Hounshell, "The Revolution Will Be Tweeted," *Foreign Policy* 187 (July/August 2011); Negar Mottahedeh, *#iranelection: Hashtag Solidarity and the Transformation of Online Life* (Stanford, CA: Stanford University Press, 2015).
4. Jonathan Haidt, "Why the Past 10 Years of American Life Have Been Uniquely Stupid," *The Atlantic* (April 11, 2022), https://www.theatlantic.com/magazine/archive/2022/05/social-media-democracy-trust-babel/629369/.
5. Chris Anderson, *The Long Tail: Why the Future of Business is Selling Less of More* (Westport, CT: Hyperion, 2006).
6. Siva Vaidyanathan, *Antisocial Media: How Facebook Disconnects Us and Undermines Democracy* (Oxford: Oxford University Press, 2018). See also Derek Thompson, "The Anti-Social Century," *The Atlantic* (February 2025), https://www.theatlantic.com/magazine/archive/2025/02/american-loneliness-personality-politics/681091/.
7. Quoted in Vaidyanathan, *Antisocial Media*, 1.
8. Jonathan Haidt, *The Anxious Generation: How the Great Rewiring of Childhood is Causing an Epidemic of Mental Illness* (London: Penguin, 2024).
9. Jean M. Twenge, *iGen: Why Today's Super-Connected Kids Are Growing Up Less Rebellious, More Tolerant, Less Happy – and Completely Unprepared for Adulthood* (New York: Atria Books, 2018). See also Hunt Allcott, Luca Braghieri, Sarah Eichmeyer, and Matthew Gentzkow, "The Welfare Effects of Social Media," *American Economic Review* 110:3 (2020), 629–76.
10. Judith Butler, quoted in Claudia Rankine, *Citizen: An American Lyric* (Minneapolis, MN: Graywolf Press, 2014), 49.
11. Judy Wajcman, "Time and Technology," in Deana A. Rohlinger and Sarah Sobieraj (eds.), *The Oxford Handbook of Digital Media Sociology* (Oxford: Oxford University Press, 2020), 9.
12. Han, *In the Swarm*, 31.

13. Sherry Turkle, *Alone Together: Why We Expect More from Technology and Less from Each Other* (New York: Basic Books, 2017 [2010]), 188.
14. Varoth Chotpitayasunondh & Karen M. Douglas. "How 'Phubbing' Becomes the Norm: The Antecedents and Consequences of Snubbing via Smartphone," *Computers in Human Behavior* 63 (2016), 9–18.
15. Russell Shaw, "Why We're Banning Phones at Our School," *The Atlantic* (August 4, 2024), https://www.theatlantic.com/ideas/archive/2024/08/phone-ban-georgetown-washington-day-school/679340/.
16. Nate Holdren, "Broken Sociality: Isolation in the Pseudo-Return to 'Pre-Pandemic Normal,'" *Peste* (February 21, 2023), https://www.pestemag.com/lost-to-follow-up/broken-sociality [https://archive.ph/H38A1].
17. Han, *In the Swarm*, 16, 54.
18. Robert Putnam, "Bowling Alone: America's Declining Social Capital," *Journal of Democracy* (January 1995), 65–78.
19. Lulu Garcia-Navarro, "The Interview: Robert Putnam Knows Why You're Lonely," *New York Times* (July 13, 2024), https://www.nytimes.com/2024/07/13/magazine/robert-putnam-interview.html
20. Jonathan Haidt and Ezra Klein, "'Our Kids are the Least Flourishing Generation We Know Of,'" *The Ezra Klein Show* (April 1, 2025), https://www.nytimes.com/2025/04/01/opinion/ezra-klein-podcast-jonathan-haidt.html.
21. Han, *In the Swarm*, 13.
22. *Ibid*., 14.
23. Ian Baucom, "Frantz Fanon's Radio: Solidarity, Diaspora, and the Tactics of Listening," *Contemporary Literature* 42:1 (2001), 15–49.
24. Han, *In the Swarm*, 16.
25. Putnam wrote: "My hunch is that meeting in an electronic forum is not the equivalent of meeting in a bowling alley – or even in a saloon – but hard empirical research is needed." Putnam, "Bowling Alone," 76.
26. Amit Katwala, "Zoom Dysmorphia is Following People into the Real World," *Wired* (August 30, 2021), https://www.wired.com/story/zoom-dysmorphia-the-real-world/.
27. Sherry Turkle, *Alone Together*.
28. Jaime E. Settle, *Frenemies: How Social Media Polarizes America* (Cambridge: Cambridge University Press, 2019); Ezra Klein, *Why We're Polarized* (New York: Simon & Schuster, 2020); Chris Bail, *Breaking the Social Media Prism: How to Make Our Platforms Less Polarizing* (Princeton, NJ: Princeton University Press, 2022).
29. Haidt, "The Past 10 Years"; see also Jonathan Haidt & Chris Bail, "Social Media and Political Dysfunction: A Collaborative Review,"

unpublished manuscript (ongoing), New York University, https://docs.google.com/document/d/1vVAtMCQnz8WVxtSNQev_e1cGmY9rnY96ecYuAj6C548/edit.

30. Cass Sunstein, *Republic.com* (Princeton, NJ: Princeton University Press, 2002).

31. "The Most Dangerous People on the Internet in 2024," *Wired* (December 30, 2024), https://www.wired.com/story/the-most-dangerous-people-on-the-internet-in-2024/. See also Renée DiResta, *Invisible Rulers: The People Who Turn Lies into Reality* (New York: PublicAffairs, 2024).

32. Cristina Criddle & Hannah Murphy, "Meta Envisages Social Media Filled with AI-Generated Users," *Financial Times* (December 26, 2024), https://www.ft.com/content/91183cbb-50f9-464a-9d2e-96063825bfcf.

33. Karen Attiah, "I Talked to Meta's Black AI Character: Here's What She Told Me," *Washington Post* (January 8, 2024), https://www.washingtonpost.com/opinions/2025/01/08/meta-ai-bots-backlash-racist/.

34. Vinson Cunningham, Naomi Fry, & Alexandra Schwartz, "Will Kids Online, In Fact, Be Alright?" *New Yorker* (November 21, 2024), https://www.newyorker.com/podcast/critics-at-large/will-kids-online-in-fact-be-all-right.

35. D. Graham Burnett and Ezra Klein, "Your Mind is Being Fracked," *The Ezra Klein Show* (May 31, 2024), https://www.nytimes.com/2024/05/31/opinion/ezra-klein-podcast-d-graham-burnett.html?showTranscript=1.

36. Shaw, "Why We're Banning Phones at Our School."

37. Natasha Singer, "Why Schools Are Racing to Ban Student Phones," *New York Times* (August 11, 2024), https://www.nytimes.com/2024/08/11/technology/school-phone-bans-indiana-louisiana.html. See also Natasha Singer, "An Epidemic of Vicious School Brawls, Fueled by Student Cellphones," *New York Times* (December 15, 2024), https://www.nytimes.com/2024/12/15/technology/school-fight-videos-student-phones.html.

38. "Governor Glenn Youngkin Issues Executive Order Establishing Cell Phone-Free Education in Virginia's K-12 Public Schools," *Governor of Virginia Official Website* (July 9, 2024), https://www.governor.virginia.gov/newsroom/news-releases/2024/july/name-1030522-en.html.

39. Hannah Ritchie, "Australia Approves Social Media Ban on Under-16s," BBC (November 28, 2024), https://www.bbc.com/news/articles/c89vjj0lxx9o.

40. Sherry Turkle, "How to Teach in an Age of Distraction," *Chronicle of Higher Education* (October 2, 2015), https://www.chronicle.com/article/how-to-teach-in-an-age-of-distraction/. See also Cal

Newport, *Deep Work: Rules for Focused Success in a Distracted World* (New York: Grand Central Publishing, 2016).

41. Sophie Bishop & Brooke Erin Duffy, "The Feminization of Social Media Labor," in Rohlinger & Sobieraj (eds.), *Oxford Handbook of Digital Media Sociology*, 482.
42. *Ibid.*, 470.
43. Brooke Erin Duffy, "How Big Tech Sells the Influencer American Dream," *Forbes* (December 20, 2024), https://www.forbes.com/sites/brookeerinduffy/2024/12/18/how-big-tech-sells-the-influencer-american-dream/. See also Brooke Erin Duffy, *(Not) Getting Paid to Do What You Love: Gender and Aspirational Labor in the Social Media Economy* (New Haven, CT: Yale University Press, 2017).
44. Faye Tsakas, "How Being an Influencer Became a New American Dream," *New York Times* (December 10, 2024), https://www.nytimes.com/2024/12/10/opinion/child-influencers-consumerism.html.
45. Burnett & Klein, "Your Mind is Being Fracked."
46. Sherry Turkle, *Reclaiming Conversation: The Power of Talk in a Digital Age* (London: Penguin, 2015), 13.
47. Burnett & Klein, "Your Mind is Being Fracked."
48. Manuel Castells, *The Rise of the Network Society*, 2nd edition (Chichester: Wiley Blackwell, 2010).
49. Sherry Turkle, "Preface to the 2017 Edition," *Alone Together: Why We Expect More from Technology and Less from Each Other* (New York: Basic Books, 2017 [2011]).
50. Carolyn Marvin, *When Old Technologies Were New: Thinking about Electric Communication in the Late Nineteenth Century* (Oxford: Oxford University Press, 1988).
51. Michael Shellenberger & Ted Nordhaus, "Evolve," *Orion* (August 25, 2011), https://orionmagazine.org/article/evolve/.
52. Bail, *Breaking the Social Media Prism*, 10.
53. Wajcman, "Time and Technology."
54. Turkle, *Alone Together*, 147.
55. Raelene Wilding, "Families, Relationships, and Technology," in Rohlinger & Sobieraj (eds.), *Oxford Handbook of Digital Media Sociology*, 151.
56. Elizabeth Fetterolf, "The Unique Magic That Happens When Two People Come Together: Allison Pugh on Building a Society of Connection," *Public Books* (June 25, 2024), https://www.publicbooks.org/the-unique-magic-that-happens-when-two-people-come-together-allison-pugh-on-building-a-society-of-connection/. See also Allison Pugh, *The Last Human Job: The Work of Connecting in a Disconnected World* (Princeton, NJ: Princeton University Press, 2024).

57. Zadie Smith, "The Dream of the Raised Arm," *New York Review of Books* (December 5, 2024), https://www.nybooks.com/articles/2024/12/05/the-dream-of-the-raised-arm-third-reich-of-dreams-beradt-zadie-smith/.
58. Teju Cole, *Tremor* (New York: Penguin Random House, 2023), 89.

5 OF COERCION

1. "Remarks by President Biden on the Covid-19 Response and the Vaccination Program," *The White House* (May 13, 2021), https://www.whitehouse.gov/briefing-room/speeches-remarks/2021/05/13/remarks-by-president-biden-on-the-covid-19-response-and-the-vaccination-program-3/; "Remarks by President Biden on Fighting the Covid-19 Pandemic," *The White House* (September 9, 2021), https://www.whitehouse.gov/briefing-room/speeches-remarks/2021/09/09/remarks-by-president-biden-on-fighting-the-covid-19-pandemic-3/.
2. "Word of the Year 2022," *Merriam-Webster* (November 29, 2022), https://www.merriam-webster.com/wordplay/word-of-the-year-2022.
3. Holdren, "Broken Sociality."
4. "Who Has the Tools? With Justin Feldman," *The Death Panel* podcast (August 18, 2022), https://www.deathpanel.net/transcripts/who-has-the-tools-with-justin-feldman.
5. David Wallace-Wells, "How Covid Remade America," *New York Times* (March 4, 2025), https://www.nytimes.com/interactive/2025/03/04/opinion/covid-impact-five-years-later.html.
6. Maynard & Simpson, *Rehearsals*, 253.
7. Rustom Bharucha, *The Second Wave: Reflections on the Pandemic through Photography, Performance and Public Culture* (Kolkata: Seagull Books, 2022), xviii.
8. Vicky Osterweil, "Remembering as an Act of Revolt," *All Cats Are Beautiful* (May 14, 2024), https://all-cats-are-beautiful.ghost.io/a-list-of-things-we-have-been-told-to-forget/.
9. Amanda Seitz, "Covid-19 Treatments to Enter the Market with a Hefty Price Tag," *Associated Press* (October 27, 2023), https://apnews.com/article/covid19-paxlovid-treatment-coronavirus-drugs-5ea6124208e915382c40303bd6d749ef.
10. Bornfree & Srinivasan, *The End Doesn't Happen All at Once.*
11. Arundhati Roy, "The Pandemic is a Portal," *Financial Times* (April 3, 2020), https://www.ft.com/content/10d8f5e8-74eb-11ea-95fe-fcd274e920ca/. See also Ragini Tharoor Srinivasan, "The Pandemic Was a Portal," *The Philosopher* (April 20, 2025), https://www.thephilosopher1923.org/post/the-pandemic-was-a-portal.

12. Grant Farred, *Only a Black Athlete Can Save Us Now* (Minneapolis: University of Minnesota Press, 2022), xxiii.
13. Pam Houston & Amy Irvine, *Air Mail: Letters of Politics, Pandemics, and Place* (Salt Lake City, UT: Torrey House Press, 2020), 113.
14. BBC Channel Four, "Letters in Lockdown," https://www.channel4.com/programmes/letters-in-lockdown.
15. Jiang Jiehong (ed.), *The Otherness of the Everyday: Twelve Conversations from the Chinese Art World during the Covid-19 Pandemic* (Bristol: Intellect, 2021).
16. Hoyt Long, Richard Jean So, & Kaitlyn Todd, "#COVID, Crisis, and the Search for Story in the Platform Age," *Critical Inquiry* 49:4 (2023), 532. See also Tizian Zumthurm and Stefan Krebs, "Collecting Middle-Class Memories? The Pandemic, Technology, and Crowdsourced Archives," *Technology and Culture* 63:2 (2022), 483–93.
17. The Black | Indigenous 100s Collective, *Say, Listen: Writing as Care* (Denver, CO: np, 2024), 17.
18. Maynard & Simpson, *Rehearsals*, 10.
19. "Together Apart," Orion Magazine, https://orionmagazine.org/2020/04/together-apart-a-new-web-series/.
20. Houston & Irvine, *Air Mail*, 15.
21. Bharucha, *Second Wave*, 202.
22. Bornfree & Srinivasan, *The End Doesn't Happen All at Once*.
23. Brad Evans, "Introduction to 'The Quarantine Files: Thinkers in Self-Isolation'," *Los Angeles Review of Books* (April 14, 2020), https://lareviewofbooks.org/article/quarantine-files-thinkers-self-isolation/.
24. Houston & Irvine, *Air Mail*, 6.
25. Butler, *What World is This?*
26. Bharucha, *Second Wave*, 203.
27. Houston & Irvine, *Air Mail*, 23; Bornfree & Srinivasan, *The End Doesn't Happen All at Once*, 30; Farred, *Only a Black Athlete*, xxv.
28. Jack Miles and Mark C. Taylor, *A Friendship in Twilight: Lockdown Conversations on Death and Life* (New York: Columbia University Press, 2022).
29. Miles & Taylor, *Friendship*, 435.
30. Maynard & Simpson, *Rehearsals*, 13.
31. *Ibid.*, 135.
32. Houston & Irvine, *Air Mail*, 1, 2, 27, 161.
33. *Ibid.*, 54, 35.
34. *Ibid.*, 34–5.
35. *Ibid.*, 97, emphasis added.

36. Robin D. G. Kelley, "Afterword," *Rehearsals*, 267.
37. Miles & Taylor, *Friendship*, 435.
38. Maynard & Simpson, *Rehearsals*, 242.
39. Kate Zambreno, *The Light Room: On Art and Care* (New York: Riverhead, 2023), 34.
40. Butler, *What World is This?*, 43.
41. Farred, *Only a Black Athlete*, xv.
42. Maynard & Simpson, *Rehearsals*, 124.
43. Houston & Irvine, *Air Mail*, 35.
44. Michelle Fishburne, *The Way We Are Now: Stories of What Americans Lost and Found during the Covid-19 Pandemic* (Chapel Hill: University of North Carolina Press, 2023), 296.
45. Butler, *What World is This?*, 8.
46. *Ibid.*, 28.
47. Christopher Schaberg, *Grounded: Perpetual Flight . . . and then the Pandemic* (Minneapolis: University of Minnesota Press, 2020), 68.
48. Zadie Smith, *Intimations: Six Essays* (London: Penguin, 2020), 7, 22.
49. *Ibid.*, 16.
50. Artie Vierkant, Beatrice Adler Bolton, & Death Panel, "'The Beyblade Strategy' or: How We Learned to Stop Worrying and Love Focused Protection," *The New Inquiry* (February 22, 2022).
51. Piotr Blumczynski & Steven Wilson, "Are We All in This Together?" in Piotr Blumczynski & Steven Wilson (eds.), *The Languages of Covid-19: Translational and Multilingual Perspectives on Global Healthcare* (Abingdon: Routledge, 2022), 1–11.
52. Beatrice Adler-Bolton & Artie Vierkant, *Health Communism* (New York: Verso, 2022), 1.
53. Fang Fang, *Wuhan Diary: Dispatches from a Quarantined City* (London: HarperCollins, 2020), 173.
54. Maynard & Simpson, *Rehearsals*, 44.
55. *Ibid.*, 39, emphasis added.
56. Houston & Irvine, *Air Mail*, 145.
57. Maynard & Simpson, *Rehearsals*, 72.
58. Rob Stein, "Is Covid Endemic Yet? Yep, Says the CDC," NPR (August 9, 2024), https://www.npr.org/sections/shots-health-news/2024/08/09/nx-s1-5060398/covid-endemic-cdc-summer-surge; Adam Kilgore, "Noah Lyle's Case Shows a New Reality for Olympians: Playing through Covid," *Washington Post* (August 9, 2024), https://www.washingtonpost.com/sports/olympics/2024/08/09/noah-lyles-covid-paris-olympics/.
59. Matthew Desmond, "Tools to End the Poverty Pandemic," *New York Review of Books* (January 18, 2024). See also Philip Rocco, "The

Waning of Pandemic Time," *Medium* (August 24, 2021), https://medium.com/3streams/the-waning-of-pandemic-time-41d56947392b.

60. Jordan Kisner, "The Unthinkable Mental Health Crisis that Shook a New England College," *New York Times* (January 22, 2024), https://www.nytimes.com/2024/01/22/magazine/worcester-polytechnic-institute-suicides.html/.
61. Beatrice Adler-Bolton, Artie Vierkant, & Jules Gill Peterson, "Covid Year Five," *The Death Panel* podcast (December 23, 2024), https://www.patreon.com/posts/118969459.

6 OF LIBERATION

1. "Abortion is Essential: Stories of Liberation," ACLU (January 21, 2022), https://www.aclu.org/news/reproductive-freedom/abortion-is-essential-stories-of-liberation/.
2. Abby Minor, *As I Said: A Dissent* (Los Angeles: Ricochet Editions, 2022), 85.
3. Heather Latimer, *Reproductive Acts: Sexual Politics in North American Fiction and Film* (Montreal: McGill-Queen's University Press, 2013), 20, emphasis added.
4. Moira Donegan, "The Pro-Choice Movement Has Won the Culture War," *The Nation* (December 16/23, 2019), https://www.thenation.com/article/archive/abortion-feminist-stigma-claws/.
5. See "We Count," from the Society of Family Planning, for more data on the post-Dobbs abortion landscape in the United States: https://societyfp.org/research/wecount/.
6. Moreover, as feminist activist Jessica Valenti documents, the anti-choice movement is increasingly emboldened to pursue total bans without any exceptions at all. See Valenti, *Abortion, Every Day* (Substack), https://jessica.substack.com.
7. For details on the restrictions and criminal sanctions imposed by HB 1280, SB 8, and the 1925 statute, see Kirk McDaniel, "Texas Trigger Ban on Abortion Goes into Effect," *Courthouse News Service* (August 25, 2022), https://www.courthousenews.com/texas-trigger-ban-on-abortion-goes-into-effect/.
8. Bryce Covert, "What It's Like to Have an Abortion Denied by Dobbs," *In These Times* (May 22, 2023), https://inthesetimes.com/article/what-its-like-to-have-an-abortion-denied/.
9. Eleanor Klibanoff & Rebecca Schneid, "Tearfully Testifying against Texas' Abortion Ban," *The Texas Tribune* (July 19, 2023), https://www.texastribune.org/2023/07/19/texas-women-testify-abortion-ban/.
10. "The Plaintiffs and Their Stories," Center for Reproductive Rights

(November 14, 2023), https://reproductiverights.org/zurawski-v-texas-plaintiffs-stories-remarks/; "Plaintiffs' Families Amicus Brief in Zurawski v. State of Texas," Center for Reproductive Rights (December 12, 2023), https://reproductiverights.org/case/zurawski-v-texas-abortion-emergency-exceptions/amicus-briefs-zurawski-v-state-of-texas/.

11. "One in Four US Women Expected to Have an Abortion in Their Lifetime," *Guttmacher* (April 17, 2024), https://www.guttmacher.org/news-release/2024/one-four-us-women-expected-have-abortion-their-lifetime/.
12. Peter Slevin, "The New Faces of Abortion Rights," *New Yorker* (August 9, 2024), https://www.newyorker.com/news/dispatch/the-new-faces-of-abortion-rights. See also Rosemary Westwood, "Women Sharing Personal Stories about Abortion Bans Have Become a Political Force," *NPR* (November 2, 2024), https://www.npr.org/sections/shots-health-news/2024/11/01/nx-s1-5157670/women-personal-story-miscarriage-reproductive-rights-abortion-bans-harris-walz-campaign.
13. Colleen Long, "Harris Ad Shows Texas Woman Who Lost Baby and Nearly Died from Sepsis amid Strict Abortion Ban," *Associated Press* (October 23, 2024), https://apnews.com/article/harris-abortion-rights-democrats-texas-trump-f5b4a28874f6abcf2a9d5eeeeb0d6d37.
14. Slevin, "New Faces of Abortion Rights."
15. Caroline Kitchener, "She Hoped Her Pregnancy Story Would Matter. Then Came Election Night," *Washington Post* (November 6, 2024), https://www.washingtonpost.com/politics/2024/11/06/georgia-woman-experience-abortion-ban/. McCallum speculates that maybe her family would have voted differently if she had "actually died," bringing to mind Gayatri Chakravorty Spivak's pithy comment that "the subaltern speaks through dying."
16. Jessica Valenti, "These Anti-abortion Lies Defined 2024," *Abortion Every Day Substack* (December 30, 2024), https://jessica.substack.com/p/these-anti-abortion-lies-defined.
17. Eva Cherniavsky, "The Canny Subaltern," in Jane Elliott & Derek Attridge (eds.), *Theory after 'Theory'* (London: Routledge, 2011), 159.
18. Rebecca Traister, "The Abortion Stories We Didn't Tell," *New York Magazine: The Cut* (July 4, 2022), https://www.thecut.com/article/rebecca-traister-post-roe-v-wade-untold-abortion-stories.html.
19. Minor, *As I Said*, 8.
20. Aria Bendix, "Woman Suing Texas over Abortion Ban Vomits on the Stand," NBC News (July 19, 2023), https://www.nbcnews.com/health/health-news/woman-suing-texas-abortion-ban-vomits-on-stand-rcna95162/.

21. "Did Biden Say Abortion Yet?" https://didbidensayabortionyet.org.
22. Margaret Ronda, Jeannette Schollaert, & Jena DiMaggio, "Introduction: Abortion Now, Abortion Forever," *Post45: Contemporaries* (June 24, 2023), https://post45.org/sections/contemporaries-essays/abortion-now-abortion-forever/.
23. Amelia Bonow & Emily Nokes, "In 'Shout Your Abortion,' a Celebration of Life," *Yes! Solutions Journalism* (January 22, 2019), https://www.yesmagazine.org/social-justice/2019/01/22/in-shout-your-abortion-a-celebration-of-life.
24. *Ours to Tell* [10:10–10:20], https://www.youtube.com/watch?v=yGSgYaBbd5Q/.
25. Margaret Ronda, "Abortion's Poetic Figures," *Post45: Contemporaries* (June 30, 2023), https://post45.org/2023/06/abortions-poetic-figures/.
26. "Could You Come Up with $400 if Disaster Struck?" *NPR* (April 23, 2016), https://www.npr.org/2016/04/24/475432149/could-you-come-up-with-400-if-disaster-struck.
27. Ragini Tharoor Srinivasan, "Three Vasectomies, or, What is an Abortion Story?" *Post45: Contemporaries* (June 25, 2023), https://post45.org/2023/06/three-vasectomies-or-what-is-an-abortion-story/.
28. Minor, *As I Said*, 85.
29. Latimer, *Reproductive Acts*, 45. See also Emre, "All Reproduction is Assisted."
30. Latimer, *Reproductive Acts*, 38.
31. Ronda, "Abortion's Poetic Figures."
32. Chimamanda Adichie, "The Danger of a Single Story," TED Talk (2020), https://www.youtube.com/watch?v=LmjKUDo7gSQ/.
33. Carly Thomsen, "The Politics of Narrative, Narrative as Politic: Rethinking Reproductive Justice Frameworks through the South Dakota Abortion Story," *Feminist Formations* 27:2 (2015), 21.
34. *Ibid.*, 13–14.
35. Quoted in *Ibid.*, 16.
36. Ronda, "Abortion's Poetic Figures."
37. Siddhartha Mitter, "Now Visiting from India, an 'Ancestor' for Everyone," *New York Times* (September 15, 2022), https://www.nytimes.com/2022/09/15/arts/design/bharti-kher-statue-central-park-india.html.
38. Juliana Spahr, "Tradition," in *That Winter the Wolf Came* (Oakland, CA: Commune Editions, 2015), 55.
39. Ronda, "Abortion's Poetic Figures."
40. Many abortion stories include reflection on what the storyteller did

and did not know, in particular about other women's experiences of abortion. As one interview subject puts it in the Planned Parenthood documentary *Ours to Tell*, "If I had known my mom had had an abortion I probably would have been able to talk to her about it. Why couldn't we talk so candidly about abortion?"

41. Thomsen, "Politics of Narrative," 21.

7 OF DIVISION

1. Rankine, *Citizen*, 42.
2. Collen Lye, "Racial Form," *Representations* 104:1 (2008), 99.
3. Michael Omi and Howard Winant, *Racial Formation in the United States*, 3rd edition (Abingdon: Routledge, 2015 [1986]), 107.
4. Omi & Winant, *Racial Formation*, 109.
5. *Ibid.*, 111.
6. Miriam Jordan, "Black Farmworkers Say They Lost Jobs to Foreigners Who Were Paid More," *New York Times* (November 12, 2021), https://www.nytimes.com/2021/11/12/us/black-farmworkers-mississippi-lawsuit.html.
7. Claudia Rankine, *Just Us: An American Conversation* (Minneapolis, MN: Graywolf Press, 2020), 76.
8. Zora Neale Hurston, quoted in Rankine, *Citizen*, 25.
9. Ragini Tharoor Srinivasan, "Ricky and Jim and Me: On Whiteness," *Politics/Letters* (January 9, 2019), http://politicsslashletters.org/features/ricky-and-jim-and-me-on-whiteness/.
10. Kamran Javadizadeh, "The Atlantic Ocean Breaking on Our Heads: Claudia Rankine, Robert Lowell, and the Whiteness of the Lyric Subject," *PMLA* 134:3 (2019), 476, 488n1.
11. Rankine, *Citizen*, 43.
12. *Ibid.*, 45.
13. Javadizadeh, "The Atlantic Ocean," 482.
14. Rankine, *Citizen*, 55.
15. Rankine, *Just Us*, 45.
16. Rankine, *Citizen*, 47.
17. Beth Loffreda & Claudia Rankine, "Introduction," in Claudia Rankine, Beth Loffreda, & Max King Cap (eds.), *The Racial Imaginary: Writers on Race in the Life of the Mind* (Fence Books, 2015), 19.
18. Rankine, *Citizen*, 43.
19. Judith Butler, *Gender Trouble* (London: Routledge, 1990), xxvi.
20. Shafak, *How to Stay Sane in an Age of Division*, 33.
21. Sylvia Brownrigg, "Looking Beyond: A Conversation with Aminatta

Forna," *LA Review of Books* (April 9, 2022), https://lareviewofbooks.org/article/looking-beyond-a-conversation-with-aminatta-forna/.

22. Quoted in Rangan *et al.*, *Thinking with an Accent*, 4–5.
23. Monica Youn, *From From* (Minneapolis, MN: Graywolf Press, 2023).
24. Loffreda & Rankine, "Introduction," 15.
25. Rankine, *Citizen*, 26.
26. *Ibid.*, 30.
27. Dorothy Roberts, *Killing the Black Body: Race, Reproduction, and the Meaning of Liberty* (New York: Vintage, 2014).
28. Edward Said, *Orientalism* (New York: Pantheon, 1978), 248.
29. Edward Said, *Culture and Imperialism* (New York: Vintage, 1993), 32.
30. *Ibid.*, 61.
31. E. M. Forster, *A Passage to India* (London: Harcourt Brace, 1924), 7.
32. *Ibid.*, 362.
33. *Ibid.*, 22.
34. *Ibid.*, 73, 76.
35. *Ibid.*, 159.
36. Said, *Orientalism*, 231.
37. Forster, *Passage*, 131.
38. Said, *Culture and Imperialism*, 191.
39. *Ibid.*, 234.
40. *Ibid.*, 235.
41. Rankine, *Just Us*, 18.
42. Forster, *Passage*, 169.
43. Said, *Orientalism*, 227.
44. Forster, *Passage*, 157.
45. *Ibid.*, 185.
46. *Ibid.*, 37.
47. *Ibid.*, 192.
48. Said, *Orientalism*, 244.
49. Rankine, *Citizen*, 14.
50. Forster, *Passage*, 15, 22.
51. Rankine, *Just Us*, 181.
52. *Ibid.*, 184.
53. *Ibid.*, 173–4.
54. *Ibid.*, 184.
55. Loffreda & Rankine, "Introduction," 13.
56. Saidiya Hartman, quoted in Rankine, *Just Us*, 132–3.
57. Rankine, *Just Us*, 170.

8 OF INCORPORATION

1. Said, *Orientalism*, xix.
2. Cole, *Tremor*, 83.
3. Teju Cole, *Every Day Is for the Thief* (New York: Random House, 2014 [2007]), 57.
4. *Ibid.*, 59, 61.
5. *Ibid.*, 62.
6. *Ibid.*, 64–6.
7. Kyla Wazana Tompkins, *Racial Indigestion: Eating Bodies in the 19th Century* (New York: NYU Press, 2012), 94.
8. C. Richard King, "The (Mis)Uses of Cannibalism in Contemporary Cultural Critique," *Diacritics* 30:1 (2000), 106–9.
9. Michel De Montaigne, Christine Bénévent, & Alain Jaubert, *Des cannibales* (Paris: Éditions Mille et Une Nuits, 2000).
10. Jennifer Brown, *Cannibalism in Literature and Film* (London: Palgrave Macmillan, 2013), 7.
11. Jack D. Forbes, *Columbus and Other Cannibals: The Wetiko Disease of Exploitation, Imperialism, and Terrorism* (full citation, 1978, reprinted 1992), 24.
12. Saidiya Hartman, *Lose Your Mother: A Journey along the Atlantic Slave Route* (New York: Farrar, Straus & Giroux, 2007), 114.
13. Daniel Boyarin, *The No-State Solution: A Jewish Manifesto* (New Haven, CT: Yale University Press, 2023), 18.
14. *Ibid.*, 20.
15. Said, *Orientalism*, xvii.
16. *Ibid.*, 3.
17. Reprinted in many places, including T. B. Macaulay, "Minute, dated 2 February 1835," *Islamic Studies* 54:3/4 (2015), 237–48. In referring to Macaulay as an Orientalist, I mean to emphasize his participation in the broad school of interpretation and body of discourse identified by Said. That said, in the Minute, Macaulay technically voices an Anglicist response to Orientalist scholars' arguments for education in Sanskrit and Arabic.
18. Said, *Orientalism*, 222, 289.
19. *Ibid.*, 4.
20. *Ibid.*, 12, emphasis added.
21. Dean MacCannell, *Empty Meeting Grounds: The Tourist Papers* (London: Routledge, 1992).
22. Lionel Shriver, "I Hope the Concept of Cultural Appropriation is a Passing Fad," *The Guardian* (September 13, 2016), https://www.theguardian.com/commentisfree/2016/sep/13/lionel-shrivers-full-

speech-i-hope-the-concept-of-cultural-appropriation-is-a-passing-fad; Zadie Smith, "Fascinated to Presume: In Defense of Fiction," *New York Review of Books* (October 24, 2019), https://www.nybooks.com/articles/2019/10/24/zadie-smith-in-defense-of-fiction/.

23. Paisley Rekdal, *Appropriate: A Provocation* (New York: Norton, 2021).
24. Micah Stack, "The G.R.I.E.F." *Oxford American* (July 23, 2015), https://oxfordamerican.org/magazine/issue-89-summer-2015/the-g-r-i-e-f.
25. Myriam Gurba, "Pendeja, You Ain't Steinbeck," *Tropics of Meta* (December 12, 2019), https://tropicsofmeta.com/2019/12/12/pendeja-you-aint-steinbeck-my-bronca-with-fake-ass-social-justice-literature/.
26. Leong, *Identity Capitalists*.
27. Deborah Root, *Cannibal Culture: Art, Appropriation, and the Commodification of Difference* (London: Routledge, 1996).
28. Cole, *Tremor*, 39.
29. For another recent novel that plays out this question, see R. F. Kuang, *Yellowface* (New York: William Morrow, 2023).
30. Cole, *Tremor*, 77–8.
31. *Ibid.*, 112.
32. Ayad Akhtar, *Disgraced* (London: Methuen Drama, 2013), 47.
33. Trinh T. Minh-ha, *Woman Native Other: Writing Postcoloniality and Feminism* (Bloomington: Indiana University Press, 1989), 48.
34. bell hooks, "Eating the Other: Desire and Resistance," *Black Looks: Race and Representation* (Boston, MA: South End Press, 1992), 368
35. *Ibid.*, 369.
36. *Ibid.*, 373.
37. Lauren Michele Jackson, "We Need to Talk about Digital Blackface in Reaction GIFs," *Teen Vogue* (August 2, 2017), https://www.teenvogue.com/story/digital-blackface-reaction-gifs.
38. Tompkins, *Racial Indigestion*.
39. Cole, *Tremor*, 167.

9 OF FORGETTING

1. Renan, "Qu'est-ce qu'une nation?," 16.
2. Rankine, *Just Us*, 293.
3. M. Mohsin Alam Bhat, "The Constitutional Case against the Citizenship Amendment Bill," *Economic and Political Weekly* 54:3 (January 19, 2019), 12–14.
4. Jules Boykoff, *What Are the Olympics For?* (Bristol: Bristol University Press, 2024).
5. Renan, "Qu'est-ce qu'une nation?," 19.

6. *Ibid.*, 11.
7. Shreeya Sinha & Mark Suppes, "Timeline of the Riots in Modi's Gujarat," *New York Times* (August 19, 2015), https://www.nytimes.com/interactive/2014/04/06/world/asia/modi-gujarat-riots-timeline.html.
8. Benedict Anderson, *Imagined Communities: Reflections on the Origin and Spread of Nationalism* (London: Verso, 1983, revised 2006), 3. See also Pheng Cheah, *Spectral Nationality: Passages of Freedom from Kant to Postcolonial Literatures of Liberation* (New York: Columbia University Press, 2003).
9. Anderson, *Imagined Communities*, 25.
10. Anderson elaborates the emergence of distinct creole, vernacular, and official nationalisms over the course of three centuries, leading up to wave of nation-states established in the mid-twentieth century anticolonial era after the Second World War.
11. Anderson, *Imagined Communities*, 201.
12. Noam Chomsky & Nathan J. Robinson, *The Myth of American Idealism: How U.S. Foreign Policy Endangers the World* (London: Hamish Hamilton, 2024), 3.
13. *Ibid.*, 5.
14. Zadie Smith, "Speaking in Tongues," *New York Review of Books* (February 26, 2009), https://www.nybooks.com/articles/2009/02/26/speaking-in-tongues-2/.
15. Boyarin, *No-State Solution*, 137n10.
16. Cole, *Tremor*, 93–4.
17. Patricia Williams, "To the North: Race, Migration, and Violence in the United States of America," *Times Literary Supplement* (April 23, 2021), 8.
18. Alicia Ostriker, "Evening in Plague Time," *The Nation*, https://www.thenation.com/article/culture/three-short-poems/.
19. J. D. Vance, *Hillbilly Elegy: A Memoir of a Family and Culture in Crisis* (New York: Harper, 2016).
20. "Are You a Racist?" JD Vance for Senate (April 5, 2022), https://www.youtube.com/watch?v=K3qYJoSV0lI.
21. Neema Avashia, "How J. D. Vance Has Written Appalachians Like Me out of His Ohio Senate Campaign," NBC News (May 3, 2022), https://www.nbcnews.com/think/opinion/jd-vance-written-appalachians-ohio-senate-campaign-rcna26933, emphasis added.
22. Quoted in Rankine, *Just Us*, 50.
23. "The 1619 Project," *New York Times* (August 2019), https://www.nytimes.com/interactive/2019/08/14/magazine/1619-america-slavery.html.
24. Pierre-Antoine Lewis, "'No People Has a Greater Claim to That Flag

than Us," *New York Times* (September 6, 2019), https://www.nytimes.com/2019/09/06/us/nikole-hannah-jones-interview.html.

25. Sean Wilentz, "A Matter of Facts," *The Atlantic* (January 22, 2020), https://www.theatlantic.com/ideas/archive/2020/01/1619-project-new-york-times-wilentz/605152/; see also Annette Gordon-Reed *et al.*, "The 1619 Project Forum," *American Historical Review* 127:4 (December 2022), 1792–873.
26. Homi Bhabha, "Introduction: Narrating the Nation," in Homi Bhabha (ed.), *Nation and Narration* (London: Routledge, 1990), 2–3.
27. Homi Bhabha, "DissemiNation: Time, Narrative, and the Margins of the Modern Nation," in Bhabha (ed.), *Nation and Narration*, 297.
28. Williams, "To the North," 7.
29. Marianne Hirsch, "Rethinking Holocaust Memory after October 7," *Public Books* (July 15, 2024).
30. Daniel Boyarin & Jonathan Boyarin, "Diaspora: Generation and the Ground of Jewish Identity," *Critical Inquiry* 19:4 (1993), 693–725.
31. Boyarin, *No-State Solution*, 3.
32. *Ibid.*, 12.
33. *Ibid.*, 29.
34. *Ibid.*, 90.
35. *Ibid.*, 97.
36. *Ibid.*, 73.
37. *Ibid.*, 47.
38. Benedict Anderson, *The Spectre of Comparisons: Nationalism, Southeast Asia, and the World* (London: Verso, 1998), 42.
39. *Ibid.*, 41.
40. *Ibid.*, 45.
41. *Ibid.*, 74.
42. *Ibid.*, 73–4.
43. Boyarin, *No-State Solution*, 93.

10 OF REMEMBERING

1. The Black | Indigenous 100s Collective, *Say, Listen*, 25.
2. Jorie Graham, *To 2040* (Port Townsend, WA: Copper Canyon Press, 2023), 45.
3. Maxine Hong Kingston, *The Woman Warrior: Memoirs of a Girlhood among Ghosts* (New York: Knopf, 1976), 8.
4. Williams, "To the North," 8.
5. Mitter, "Now Visiting from India, an 'Ancestor' for Everyone."
6. The Black | Indigenous 100s Collective, *Say, Listen*, 64.

7. Amitav Ghosh, *The Great Derangement: Climate Change and the Unthinkable* (Chicago: University of Chicago Press, 2016), 92. See also Roy Scranton, *Impasse: Climate Change and the Limits of Progress* (Stanford University Press, 2025).
8. Anna Lowenhaupt Tsing, *The Mushroom at the End of the World: On the Possibility of Life in Capitalist Ruins* (Princeton, NJ: Princeton University Press, 2015), 1–2.
9. *Ibid.*, 2.
10. Amitav Ghosh, "Brutes," *Orion* (Autumn 2021), 57.
11. Amitav Ghosh, *The Nutmeg's Curse: Parables for a Planet in Crisis* (Chicago, IL: University of Chicago Press, 2021), 14, 82.
12. *Ibid.*, 198. Ghosh writes: "It may appear self-evident to humans that they are the gardeners who decide what happens to trees. Yet, on a different timescale, it might appear equally evident that trees are gardening humans."
13. Jane Bennett, *Vibrant Matter: A Political Ecology of Things* (Durham, NC: Duke University Press, 2020).
14. Tsing, *Mushroom*, 22.
15. Ghosh, *Nutmeg's Curse*, 30, 33.
16. Tsing, *Mushroom*, 47; Sumana Roy, *How I Became a Tree* (New Haven, CT: Yale University Press, 2021); Hannah Knox, *Thinking Like a Climate: Governing a City in Times of Environmental Change* (Durham, NC: Duke University Press, 2020); Mel Chen, *Animacies: Biopolitics, Racial Mattering, and Queer Affect* (Durham, NC: Duke University Press, 2012).
17. Marisol de la Cadena, *Earth Beings: Ecologies of Practice across Andean Worlds* (Durham, NC: Duke University Press, 2015); Eduardo Kohn, *How Forests Think: Toward an Anthropology beyond the Human* (Oakland: University of California Press, 2013).
18. Reid Gómez, *The Web of Differing Versions: Where Africa Ends and America Begins* (Minneapolis: University of Minnesota Press, 2025).
19. Maynard & Simpson, *Rehearsals*, 204.
20. Timothy Morton, "Rejecting the Anthropocene is a Mistake," iaiNews (April 9, 2024), https://iai.tv/articles/rejecting-the-anthropocene-is-a-mistake-auid-2806.
21. Srinivas Aravamudan, "The Catachronism of Climate Change," *Diacritics* 41:3 (2013), 7.
22. Jedediah Purdy, *After Nature: A Politics for the Anthropocene* (Cambridge, MA: Harvard University Press, 2015), 50.
23. Jason W. Moore, "The Rise of Cheap Nature," in Jason W. Moore (ed.), *Anthropocene or Capitalocene? Nature, History, and the Crisis of Capitalism* (Oakland, CA: PM Press, 2016), 82.

24. Dipesh Chakrabarty, "Afterword," *South Atlantic Quarterly* 116:1 (2017), 167–8.
25. Dipesh Chakrabarty, "Postcolonial Studies and Climate Change," *New Literary History* 43:1 (2012), 10.
26. Ghosh, "Brutes," 56.
27. Naomi Klein & Astra Taylor, "The Rise of End Times Fascism," *The Guardian* (April 13, 2025), https://www.theguardian.com/us-news/ng-interactive/2025/apr/13/end-times-fascism-far-right-trump-musk.
28. As I type these words on January 10, 2025, the city of Los Angeles is on fire. The news is full of images of devastated neighborhoods in Malibu, Pacific Palisades, and Altadena, including charred celebrity mansions and disappeared beachfront chateaus. Viewed without context, the scenes resemble the ruined landscape of Gaza, its structures annihilated by US-made bombs. World-endings, redux.
29. Ghosh, *Great Derangement*, 111.
30. Natalie Diaz, "Eastbound, Soon," from "Envelopes of Air," *New Yorker* (May 23, 2018), https://www.newyorker.com/books/poems/envelopes-of-air-ada-limon-and-natalie-diaz-forge-a-bond-amid-the-shifting-landscape-of-contemporary-america.
31. Graham, *To 2040*, 17.
32. *Ibid.*, 77.
33. Aravamudan, "Catachronism," 8.
34. Graham, *To 2040*, 5.
35. *Ibid.*, 6.
36. *Ibid.*, 7.
37. *Ibid.*, 27.
38. *Ibid.*, 19.
39. *Ibid.*, 21–2.
40. *Ibid.*, 22–3.
41. *Ibid.*, 45.
42. *Ibid.*, 34.
43. Christian Wessels, "Just Now and Gone: On Jorie Graham's *To 2040*," *Cleveland Review of Books* (August 17, 2023), https://www.clereviewofbooks.com/writing/jorie-graham-to-2040.
44. Ghosh, *Great Derangement*, 4–5.
45. Quoted in Brian Blanchfield, *Proxies: Essays Near Knowing* (New York: Nightboat Books, 2016), 177.
46. Cole, *Tremor*, 28–9.
47. *Ibid.*, 29.
48. Michael Schwarz, "Global Démos without Krátos? Democratic

Cosmopolitics and the Role of the World Parliament in Habermas's Model of a Global Constitutional Order," unpublished manuscript.

49. Michaela Bronstein, "Taking the Future into Account: Today's Novels for Tomorrow's Readers," *PMLA* 134:1 (2019), 122. The Future Library currently contains books by authors including Margaret Atwood, Tsitsi Dangarembga, Han Kang, Karl Ove Knausgaard, Elif Shafak, Sjón, and Ocean Vuong.
50. Sara Marcus, *Political Disappointment: A Cultural History from Reconstruction to the AIDS Crisis* (Cambridge, MA: Harvard University Press, 2023), 1.
51. *Ibid.*, 16. Cf. Lauren Berlant, *Cruel Optimism* (Durham, NC: Duke University Press, 2012).
52. Marcus, *Political Disappointment*, 1.
53. *Ibid.*, 194–5.
54. *Ibid.*, 12, 19.
55. Vicky Osterweil, "Remembering as an Act of Revolt," *All Cats Are Beautiful* (March 14, 2024), https://all-cats-are-beautiful.ghost.io/a-list-of-things-we-have-been-told-to-forget/.
56. Graham, *To 2040*, 83.

Index